# Collins

# Maths

## Age 5 – 7

## Key Stage 1

### SATs Study Book

# KS1 Maths

## SATs Study Book

Ian Dobbs and
e Hutchinson

# Contents

# Contents

# Numbers and Counting

- Understand what a number is
- Count from 0–20 in numbers and words
- Count to 100

## Numbers

A **number** is a symbol used to **count** how many there are of something.

Numbers are odd or even. 2, 4, 6 and 8 are even and 1, 3, 5 and 7 are odd.

| 1 | 2 | 3 | 4 | 5 |
|---|---|---|---|---|
| One | Two | Three | Four | Five |
| 6 | 7 | 8 | 9 | 10 |
| Six | Seven | Eight | Nine | Ten |
| 11 | 12 | 13 | 14 | 15 |
| Eleven | Twelve | Thirteen | Fourteen | Fifteen |
| 16 | 17 | 18 | 19 | 20 |
| Sixteen | Seventeen | Eighteen | Nineteen | Twenty |

Each number has a **value**:

A single-**digit** number is any number between 0 and 9.

A two-digit number is any number between 10 and 99.

The single-digit number with the least value is 0.

The two-digit number with the most value is 99.

**Key Point**

Remember that 0, 1, 2, 3, 4, 5, 6, 7, 8 and 9 are the only single-digit numbers.

## Counting

Counting is a way of finding an amount and knowing which number shows that amount.

Each number must follow an **order** or **sequence**:
- The number that has the least value in a sequence is 0.
- Each number above 0 has more value in the sequence.

**Key Point**

You can count a sequence forwards or backwards but the order of the numbers stays the same.

Numbers are arranged in a sequence according to value:

0  1  2  3  4  5  6  7  8  9

Least to most value – single-digit numbers

10  11  12  13  14  15  16  17  18  19  20

Least to most value – two-digit numbers to 20

- Here are 11 fish.

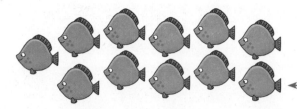

- If two more fish join them, count on two more to get 13.

**Study**

The symbol to show the number of fish is 11.

The symbol to show the number of fish now is 13.

# Counting to 100

You need to be able to count to 100. This number square will help you to learn the positions of the numbers from 0–99.

| 0 | 1 | 2 | 3 | 4 | 5 | 6 | 7 | 8 | 9 |
|---|---|---|---|---|---|---|---|---|---|
| 10 | 11 | 12 | 13 | 14 | 15 | 16 | 17 | 18 | 19 |
| 20 | 21 | 22 | 23 | 24 | 25 | 26 | 27 | 28 | 29 |
| 30 | 31 | 32 | 33 | 34 | 35 | 36 | 37 | 38 | 39 |
| 40 | 41 | 42 | 43 | 44 | 45 | 46 | 47 | 48 | 49 |
| 50 | 51 | 52 | 53 | 54 | 55 | 56 | 57 | 58 | 59 |
| 60 | 61 | 62 | 63 | 64 | 65 | 66 | 67 | 68 | 69 |
| 70 | 71 | 72 | 73 | 74 | 75 | 76 | 77 | 78 | 79 |
| 80 | 81 | 82 | 83 | 84 | 85 | 86 | 87 | 88 | 89 |
| 90 | 91 | 92 | 93 | 94 | 95 | 96 | 97 | 98 | 99 |

100

**Tip**

Look for patterns in the number square. For example, the numbers increase by 10 down each column.

## Quick Test

1. a) Write the word for the number 4.  *four*
   b) Write the number symbol for thirteen. *13*

2. Circle the number in this list that has the lowest value and circle the number that has the highest value.

   (16)   17   18   19   (20)

3. Write the missing numbers in the spaces.

| 1 | 2 | 3 | 4 | 5 | 6 | 7 | 8 | 9 | 10 |
|---|---|---|---|---|---|---|---|---|---|
| 11 | 12 | 13 | 14 | 15 | 16 | 17 | 18 | 19 | 20 |

**Key Words**

- Number
- Count
- Value
- Digit
- Order
- Sequence

5

# Counting Forwards and Backwards

- Count forwards and backwards
- Use number patterns

## Counting Forwards

When you count **forwards**, you start with a number of lower value and move on to numbers with a higher value.

| 0 | 1 | 2 | 3 | 4 | 5 | 6 | 7 | 8 | 9 |
|---|---|---|---|---|---|---|---|---|---|

This is counting forwards using single-digit numbers.

| 10 | 11 | 12 | 13 | 14 | 15 | 16 | 17 | 18 | 19 | 20 |
|---|---|---|---|---|---|---|---|---|---|---|

This is counting forwards using two-digit numbers from 10 to 20.

### Example

Sarah had 25 sweets in her bag. She added five more. How many sweets did Sarah then have?

Start at 25. Count on 5 = 30 sweets.

**Key Point**

Numbers are ordered according to their value.

## Counting Backwards

When you count **backwards**, you start with a number of higher value and move back to numbers with a lower value.

| 9 | 8 | 7 | 6 | 5 | 4 | 3 | 2 | 1 | 0 |
|---|---|---|---|---|---|---|---|---|---|

This is counting backwards using single-digit numbers.

| 20 | 19 | 18 | 17 | 16 | 15 | 14 | 13 | 12 | 11 | 10 |
|---|---|---|---|---|---|---|---|---|---|---|---|

This is counting to a lower value using two-digit numbers between 10 and 20.

## Example

Here are eight small frogs. If four of them jump away, how many frogs are left?

Start at 8. Count back 4 = 4 frogs.

# Number Patterns

You can count forwards and backwards in steps of 2, 3, 5 and 10.

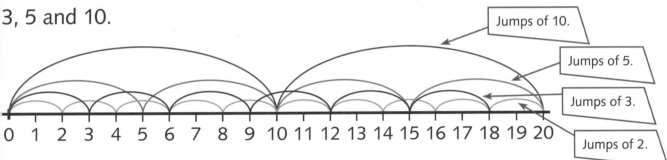

Jumps of 10.

Jumps of 5.

Jumps of 3.

Jumps of 2.

0 1 2 3 4 5 6 7 8 9 10 11 12 13 14 15 16 17 18 19 20

## Key Point

Numbers always stay in the same order but can be counted backwards or forwards.

## Quick Test

**1.** Write the missing numbers on the snake.

**2.** Start at 19 and count back the given amounts.

**a)** Count back 5 = 14

**b)** Count back 11 = 8

**3.** There are five kittens asleep in a basket. If four of them wake up and go outside to play, how many kittens are still asleep in the basket? 1

## Key Words

• Forwards
• Backwards

# Counting in Steps of 2, 3, 5 and 10

- Count in steps of 2, 3 and 5 from zero, and in 10s from any number, forwards and backwards

## Counting in Steps of 2 and 10

When counting in **steps** of 2, you miss out each **alternate** number.

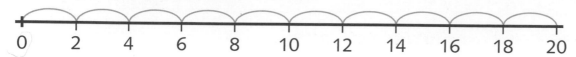

### Example

Imagine you had 20 apples and each is in a **pair** of 2. You could count the apples in steps of 2.

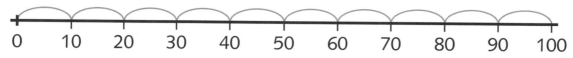

Ten lots of 2 is 20 apples.

You can count in steps of 10.

### Example

If you have two boxes of sandwiches and each box holds 10 sandwiches, that would be two **lots of** 10, or 20 sandwiches, in total.

**Key Point**

You can count in steps of 10 from any number.

Four lots of 10 is 40 sandwiches.

If you found two more boxes, how many sandwiches would you have now?   40      56

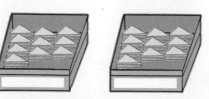

# Counting in Steps of 3 and 5

A step of 3 is one lot of 3. Numbers can be counted in steps of 3.

- Starting at 0, the first step of 3 would be 3 and the next would be 6.
- You can start at any number and count forwards or backwards in steps of 3.

### Example

If you had 27 pencils in a case and added three more, you would start at 27 and count on one step of 3. You would then have 30 pencils.

A step of 5 is one lot of 5. Numbers can be counted forwards or backwards in steps of 5.

| 0 | 5 | 10 | 15 | 20 | 25 | 30 | ← Least to most value. |
|---|---|----|----|----|----|----|------------------------|

| 30 | 25 | 20 | 15 | 10 | 5 | 0 | ← Most to least value. |
|----|----|----|----|----|---|---|------------------------|

### Example

There are 15 snails grouped into lots of 3. You can count them in steps of 3. There are five lots which is 15 snails in **total**.

**Key Point**

You can count in steps of 3 or 5 starting at any number.

---

## Quick Test

1. You have two pairs of socks and you get three more pairs. How many individual socks do you have? 10
2. Write in the missing numbers counting in lots of 10.

| 34 | 44 | 54 | 64 | 74 | 84 | 94 |
|----|----|----|----|----|----|----|

3. Count back in steps of 10 to fill in the missing numbers.

| 72 | 62 | 52 | 42 | 32 | 20 | 12 |
|----|----|----|----|----|----|----|

**Key Words**

- Step
- Alternate
- Pair
- Lots of
- Total

# More and Less

- Use symbols to show the relationship between the value of two numbers
- Identify one more or one less than a given number

## What is More? What is Less?

**More** means a **higher** number value. **Less** means a **lower** number value. Each number has a value.

- A number that has a higher value is further up the number sequence.
- A number that has a lower value is further down the number sequence.

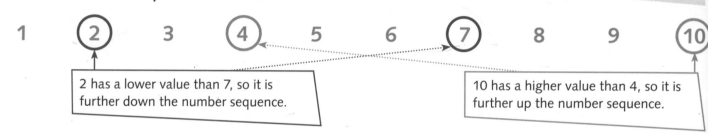

2 has a lower value than 7, so it is further down the number sequence.

10 has a higher value than 4, so it is further up the number sequence.

| 10 | 20 | 30 | 40 | 50 | 60 | 70 | 80 | 90 | 100 |
|-----|--------|--------|-------|-------|-------|---------|--------|--------|-------------|
| Ten | Twenty | Thirty | Forty | Fifty | Sixty | Seventy | Eighty | Ninety | One hundred |

20 has a lower value than 30, so it is further down the number sequence.

90 has a higher value than 70, so it is further up the number sequence.

### Key Point

When you make a number greater, you are adding. When you make a number smaller, you are subtracting.

## Useful Symbols

You can use symbols to show the value of one number when compared to another number.

- The symbol < means 'is less than'.
- The symbol > means 'is more than'.
- The symbol = means 'is **equal** to'.

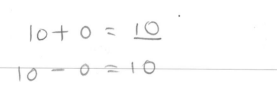

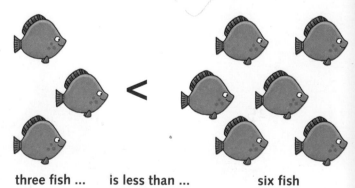

three fish ...    is less than ...    six fish

10

## Example

**10 < 20** ← 10 is less than 20.

**45 > 44** ← 45 is more than 44.

**70 = 70** ← 70 is equal to 70.

# One More, One Less

To find numbers that are one more, and one less, first choose a number. Then find the number that is the next one forwards in the sequence and the number that is one backwards.

5   6   7   ← 7 is one more than 6; 5 is one less than 6.

65  66  67  ← 67 is one more than 66; 65 is one less than 66.

### Key Point

If you know the correct sequence of numbers, you can find one more, or one less, of a given number.

## Example

Here are three biscuits. What would be one more biscuit and one less biscuit?

One more than three biscuits would be four biscuits.

One less than three biscuits would be two biscuits.

### Tip

When you add or subtract zero, the starting number remains the same.

## Quick Test

**1.** Write one more and one less.

| 4 | 5 | 6 |   | 6 | 7 | 8 |   | 3 | 4 | 5 |

**2.** Put these numbers in order from least to most:

3    45    21    19    35    3, 19, 21, 35, 45

**3.** Use < or > to show the values of these numbers.

**a)** 16 > 9   **b)** 0 < 2   **c)** 98 > 32

### Key Words
• More
• Higher
• Less
• Lower
• Equal

11

# Place Value

- Understand place value in two-digit numbers
- Partition a two-digit number

## What Does Place Value Mean?

**Place value** means that the value of a digit changes, due to where it is placed within the number.

A two-digit number, such as 34, is made out of two digits, a 3 and a 4.

Because the 3 is before the 4, its place makes it **worth** more. The 3 is worth 30.

**So, 34 is really 30 and 4!**

When you split a number into each digit's value, it is called **partitioning**.

### Example

If these numbers were partitioned, then they would look like this:

$$56 = 50 + 6 \qquad 12 = 10 + 2 \qquad 78 = 70 + 8$$

**Key Point**

Remember that in two-digit numbers, the final digit is always the **units** and the first digit is always the lots of 10.

### Quick Test

1. Partition these two-digit numbers.

   a) 65 = [60] + [5]     c) 13 = [10] + [3]

   b) 48 = [40] + [8]     d) 77 = [70] + [7]

2. Put these partitioned numbers back together.

   a) 30 + 5 = [35]   b) 60 + 9 = [69]   c) 50 + 1 = [51]

**Key Words**

- Place value
- Worth
- Partitioning
- Units

# Practice Questions

## Challenge 1

Use the number line to help with this test.

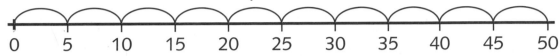

0  5  10  15  20  25  30  35  40  45  50

1  Write the missing numbers counting in steps of 5.

| 5 | 10 | 15 | 20 | 25 | 30 |

3 marks

## Challenge 2

1  Put these partitioned numbers back together.

a)  30 + 4 = _34_

b)  60 + 7 = _67_

c)  70 + 8 = _78_

d)  90 + 9 = _99_

4 marks

2  Put these numbers in order from least to most.

87     54     100     23     2     16     44

_2, 16, 23, 44, 54, 87, 100_

1 mark

3  Circle the odd numbers in this list.

 (23)    14    (45)    (5)    16    (13)    98

1 mark

## Challenge 3

1  Write the missing numbers using steps of 3. Look at the order first!

1 mark

27    18    15    12    9    6

2  Partition these two-digit numbers.

a)  95 = _90_ + _5_

b)  17 = _10_ + _7_

2 marks

3  Write a number that comes between these numbers.

a)  23 _25_ 33

b)  12 _16_ 19

2 marks

## Solving Number Problems

- Understand number facts
- Solve one-step problems involving addition and subtraction
- Solve missing number problems

# What is a Number Fact?

A number **fact** is a pair of numbers that equal an amount. **Different** pairs of numbers can equal the same amount.

All possible pairs that add or subtract to the same amount are known as facts for that amount.

These are the addition number facts that total 10. Learn these and you will be able to solve many **problems** using numbers up to 100.

| | | |
|---|---|---|
| 0 + 10 = 10 | 4 + 6 = 10 | 8 + 2 = 10 |
| 1 + 9 = 10 | 5 + 5 = 10 | 9 + 1 = 10 |
| 2 + 8 = 10 | 6 + 4 = 10 | 10 + 0 = 10 |
| 3 + 7 = 10 | 7 + 3 = 10 | |

**Key Point**

There are many more subtraction facts. For example:

11 − 1 = 10
12 − 2 = 10
13 − 3 = 10

### Example

Look at the teddies.

They are helping us with a number fact of 10:
3 + 7 = 10

There are 10 teddies in total. If you do the calculation as a subtraction, this is what it would look like: 10 − 7 = 3

Look at these number sentences:

$3 + 7 = 10$  $10 - 7 = 3$

Now imagine that there are 30 teddies and 70 teddies in separate groups. The calculation would look like this:

$30 + 70 = 100$ or $70 + 30 = 100$

There are 100 teddies in total.

If you do the calculation as a subtraction, this is what it would look like: $100 - 70 = 30$

Look at these number sentences:

$30 + 70 = 100$  $100 - 70 = 30$

Can you see the way adding a zero works?

# Number Problems

A number problem is a sum that needs to be answered. Addition and subtraction can be used.

- Addition is the **inverse** or opposite of subtraction.
- Addition sums use + (add) and = (equals).
- Subtraction sums use − (minus) and = (equals).
- Pictures can be used to help you solve problems.

$40 + 60 = 100$
$4 + 6 = 100$
$3 \times 10 = 30$

**Quick Test**

1. Look at the balloons and make your own addition or subtraction number sentence. $4 + 6 = 10$ $10 - 4 = 6$ $6 + 4 = 10$ $10 - 6 = 4$

2. Answer these missing number problems.

a) $\boxed{1} + 15 = 16$   b) $20 = 10 + \boxed{10}$

c) $23 - \boxed{5} = 18$   d) $12 = 20 - \boxed{8}$

## Using Two-Digit Numbers

- Read, write and understand the use of +, – and =
- Add and subtract one-digit and two-digit numbers

# A Two-Digit Number and Ones

Adding a ones number (unit) to a two-digit number is easy! Always start with the larger number and count on **forwards** with the smaller number.

### Example

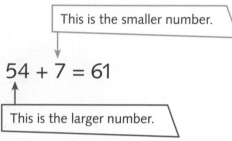

This is the smaller number.

$$54 + 7 = 61$$

This is the larger number.

Find 54 on a number square or hold the number in your head. Now count forwards 7 ones to get 61.

Subtracting a ones number from a two-digit number is the same but in reverse. Always start with the larger number and count **backwards** with the smaller number.

### Example

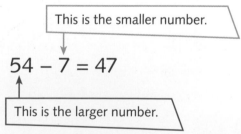

This is the smaller number.

$$54 - 7 = 47$$

This is the larger number.

Find 54 on a number square or hold the number in your head. Now count backwards 7 ones to get 47.

**Tip**

You could draw your own number line to fit around any addition or subtraction sum you wish to solve.

# Using Two Two-Digit Numbers

When a number problem uses two two-digit numbers, you break down the sum into tens and units.

**Example**

Start by adding just the tens:

$$43 + 26 =$$

4 tens  2 tens
(= 40)  (= 20)

4 tens + 2 tens = 6 tens or 40 + 20 = **60**

Then add the units:

$$43 + 26 =$$

3 units   6 units

3 + 6 = **9**

Now add both of the answers together:

60 + 9 = **69**

When you subtract a two-digit number from a two-digit number, start with the tens of the smaller number:

2 units

$$56 - 42 =$$

4 tens of the smaller number

Now count back 4 tens from the bigger number:

56 count back 4 tens: 56 46 36 26 **16**

Finally, use your answer and count back the units:

16 − 2 = **14**

## Quick Test

**1.** Solve these addition sums.

   **a)** 33 + 4 = _37_       **b)** 82 + 9 = _91_

**2.** Solve these subtraction sums.

   **a)** 87 − 5 = _82_       **b)** 76 − 4 = _72_

**Key Point**

The first number in a two-digit number is the tens number and the second number is the ones/units number.

**Key Point**

You can only subtract a smaller number from a larger number.

**Tip**

Use a 100 square to help you count forwards and backwards in tens.

**Key Words**

- Forwards
- Backwards

# Practice Questions

## Challenge 1

1 Look at the bees. Find all ten addition number facts for the total number of bees.

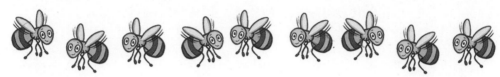

| | | | | |
|---|---|---|---|---|
| 0+9=9 | 1+8=9 | 2+7=9 | 3+6=9 | 4+5=9 |
| 5+4=9 | 6+3=9 | 7+2=9 | 8+1=9 | 9+0=9 |

10 marks: 10

## Challenge 2

10 − 6 = 4

1 What is the inverse of 6 + 4 = 10? ~~10 − 6 = 4~~

1 mark: 0

2 What is the inverse of 20 – 10 = 10? 10 + 10 = 20

10 + 10 = 20

1 mark: 0

## Challenge 3

1 Answer the following missing number problems.

a) 9 + 1 = 10 ✓ b) 8 + 11 = 19 ✓

c) 20 = 3 + 17 ✓ d) 14 = 5 + 9 ✓

4 marks: 4

2 How many bottles would you need to add to have a total of 15 bottles?

10 ✓

1 mark: 1



15/17

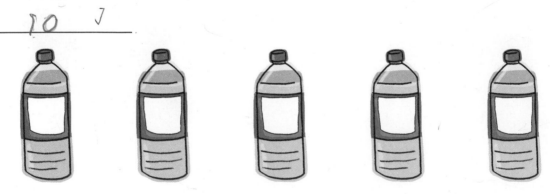

1   There are 10 cookies on a plate and you eat three of them.

Count back to find how many cookies are left.   _7_

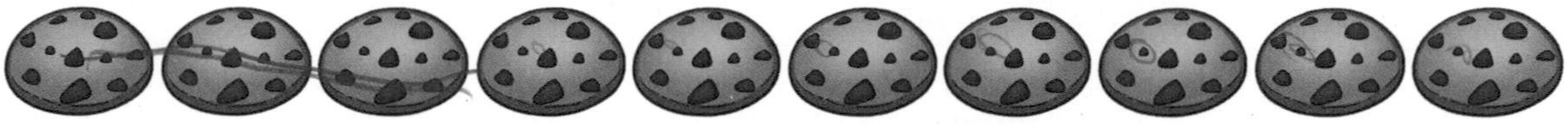

1 mark

2   Put these numbers in order of value from least to most.

8, 17, 3, 25, 56, 69, 0, 54, 71

_0, 3, 8, 17, 25, 54, 56, 69, 71_
1 mark

3   Which group has fewer buttons?

Group A

Group B

Group _B_
1 mark

4   Partition these two-digit numbers.

a)  23
_20+3=23_

b)  47
_40+7=47_

c)  99
_90+9=99_

d)  13
_10+3=13_
4
4 marks

5   These stepping stones are counting on to 100. Write the missing numbers on the stones so that they are in the correct sequence.

| 94 | 95 | 96 | 97 | 98 | 99 | 100 |

1 mark

8

# Multiplication

- Recall and use multiplication facts of 2, 5 and 10
- Use the symbols × and = in a calculation
- Use arrays and repeated addition to solve multiplication problems

## Multiplication

Multiplication means lots of, or times. Multiplication is repeated addition. It is like adding the same number lots of times.

Multiplication is an **operation**. It is shown by the symbol ×.

- To multiply, a single number is counted in lots of that number.
- A multiplication using two numbers can be done in any order and still have the same answer. This means multiplication is commutative.
- The numbers that are multiplied are called **factors**. The answer is called the **product**.

**Key Point**

A multiplication of two factors can be done in any order and still give the same product.

### Example

$5 \times 2 = 10$

$2 \times 5 = 10$

So 5 × 2 is five lots of two and 2 × 5 is two lots of five, but the answer, or product, is the same.

A picture that represents a multiplication is called an **array**.

## Example

This array shows the multiplication 8 × 2 = 16.

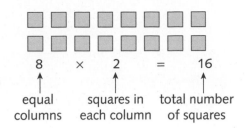

| 8 | × | 2 | = | 16 |

equal columns | squares in each column | total number of squares

A set of the same number being multiplied is called a times table.

You need to know your 2, 5 and 10 times tables.

| | | |
|---|---|---|
| 1 × 2 = 2 | 1 × 5 = 5 | 1 × 10 = 10 |
| 2 × 2 = 4 | 2 × 5 = 10 | 2 × 10 = 20 |
| 3 × 2 = 6 | 3 × 5 = 15 | 3 × 10 = 30 |
| 4 × 2 = 8 | 4 × 5 = 20 | 4 × 10 = 40 |
| 5 × 2 = 10 | 5 × 5 = 25 | 5 × 10 = 50 |
| 6 × 2 = 12 | 6 × 5 = 30 | 6 × 10 = 60 |
| 7 × 2 = 14 | 7 × 5 = 35 | 7 × 10 = 70 |
| 8 × 2 = 16 | 8 × 5 = 40 | 8 × 10 = 80 |
| 9 × 2 = 18 | 9 × 5 = 45 | 9 × 10 = 90 |
| 10 × 2 = 20 | 10 × 5 = 50 | 10 × 10 = 100 |

## Example

Here are four lots of two buttons. Four lots of two equals eight buttons in total.

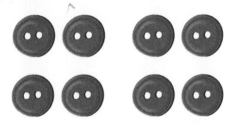

**Tip**

The multiplication 4 × 2 is repeated addition of 2 + 2 + 2 + 2. They both equal 8!

## Quick Test

**1.** Look at these repeated additions and write them as multiplications.

a) 2 + 2 + 2 = 6          | 5 | × | 2 | = | 6 | ✓

b) 5 + 5 = 10             | 2 | × | 5 | = | 10 | ✓

c) 10 + 10 + 10 + 10 = 40 | 4 | × | 10 | = | 40 | ✓

**Key Words**

- Operation
- Factor
- Product
- Array

21

## Division

• Use the symbols ÷ and = in a calculation
• Solve problems involving division using a variety of methods

# Division

Division means to **share** into equal amounts. Division is an operation. It is shown by the symbol ÷.

• When you **divide**, a **larger** number is shared so that each **amount** is the same.
• When you divide, the numbers cannot be divided in any order. Division is not commutative.
• **Odd** numbers such as 1, 3, 5 and 7 cannot be divided **equally** into whole numbers.

**Key Point**

Odd numbers cannot be divided equally into whole numbers.

### Example

If two people shared four sweets, it would mean that they got two sweets each.

The sum to show this would be:

$4 ÷ 2 = 2$

**Key Point**

Remember that you always divide the larger number by the smaller number. They cannot be switched around.

The result of sharing a number into more divisions means that the amount in each share gets **smaller**.

## Dividing Into Equal Parts

When you divide any number by 2, you halve its value.

• 4 divided by 2 = 2
• 20 divided by 2 = 10
• 100 divided by 2 = 50

## Example

Look at the pizza. If the whole pizza was shared by two people, they would get five slices each. If the pizza was shared by five people, they would only get two slices each.

The **calculation** would look like this:

$10 \div 2 = 5$

$10 \div 5 = 2$

## Quick Test

**1. a)** You and your friend have 10 strawberries. Divide them so that each of you has the same amount. How many strawberries would you each get? 5

    **b)** If you shared the strawberries between five people, how many would they each get? 2

    **c)** If you shared the strawberries between 10 people, how many would they each get? 1

**2.** Now look at the answers to question 1 a), b) and c) and write the calculation you did using ÷ and =.

| a) | 10 | ÷ | 2 | = | 5 |
|---|---|---|---|---|---|
| b) | 10 | ÷ | 5 | = | 2 |
| c) | 10 | ÷ | 10 | = | 1 |

**Key Words**

- Share
- Divide
- Larger
- Amount
- Odd
- Equally
- Smaller
- Calculation

23

# Connecting Multiplication and Division

- Show that multiplication is the inverse of division and use this to check calculations
- Solve problems involving multiplication and division using a variety of methods
- Doubling and halving numbers

## Multiplication and Division

Multiplication and division are opposite.

- When you multiply the result has a higher product.
- When you divide the result is always lower.

You can check your work by doing a multiplication and division using the same numbers.

### Example

Look at the four chickens. This calculation as a multiplication would be:

$2 \times 2 = 4$

Two lots of two chickens equals four chickens in total.

Using the same numbers as a division (inverse) would be:

$4 \div 2 = 2$

So, four chickens divided by 2 equals two chickens.

## Doubling and Halving

When you multiply any number by 2, you **double** its value.

When you divide any number by 2, you **halve** its value.

> ### Key Point
> Division is the inverse or opposite of multiplication. Multiplication is the inverse of division.

> ### Tip
> Use multiplication to check your division answer and use division to check your multiplication answer.

## Example

Here are six ice-creams.

If you multiply the number of ice-creams by 2, you double the number of ice-creams to 12:

6 × 2 = 12

If you then divide the 12 ice-creams by 2, you halve the number of ice-creams to 6:

12 ÷ 2 = 6

**Key Point**

Halving is the inverse of doubling.

## Quick Test

**1.** Double the number of dice by multiplying them by 2.

4 × 2 = 8    groups    4

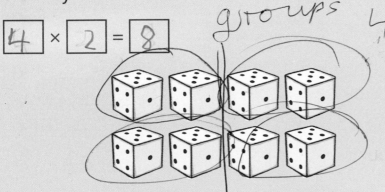

**2.** Halve the number of dice in question 1 by dividing them by 2.

8 ÷ 4 = 2

**3.** Colour this array to show the calculation 5 × 2 = 10.

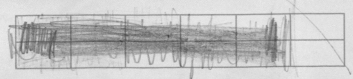

**4.** What are the two factors in this multiplication?

3 × 5 = 15    3 and 5

**Tip**

Always start with the highest value number when dividing.

**Key Words**

• Double
• Halve

## Practice Questions

**Challenge 1**

1   Complete the times tables.

| 7 × 2 = 14 ✓ | 3 × 5 = 15 ✓ | 1 × 10 = 10 ✓ |
|---|---|---|
| 3 × 2 = 6 ✓ | 6 × 5 = 30 ✓ | 5 × 10 = 50 ✓ |
| 5 × 2 = 10 ✓ | 10 × 5 = 50 ✓ | 7 × 10 = 70 ✓ |
| 10 × 2 = 20 ✓ | 2 × 5 = 10 ✓ | 10 × 10 = 100 ✓ |

4 marks

2   Write the calculation for double and half the number of pears.

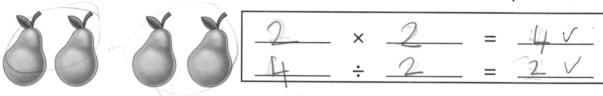

| 2 | × | 2 | = | 4 ✓ |
|---|---|---|---|---|
| 4 | ÷ | 2 | = | 2 ✓ |

2 marks

4

**Challenge 2**

PS   1   If Kari had 10 bananas and she shared them equally with her friend, how many bananas would they have each?

_____ 5 ✓ _____

1 mark

PS   2   a)  If one pizza has six slices, how many slices would two pizzas have?

_____ 12 ✓ _____

1 mark

b)  Write the calculation.

_____ 6 + 6 = 12 ✓ _____
2 × 6 = 12

1 mark

**Challenge 3**

1   a)  Write this repeated addition as a multiplication. or  5 × 2 = 10

2 + 2 + 2 + 2 + 2 = 10       2 2 × 10 = 20 × 2 = 10

1 mark

b)  Write the inverse of this multiplication.

5 × 4 = 20       20 20 5 ÷ 4 = 5

1 mark

1  Order these numbers from least to most according to their value.

23  2  45  17  89  16  98  10

2  10  16  17  23  45  89  98

1 mark

2  Write one more and one less of these numbers.

a)

| 66 | 67 | 68 | ✓

b)

| 44 | 45 | 46 | ✓

c)

| 11 | 12 | 13 | ✓

d)

| 20 | 21 | 22 | ✓

e)

| 29 | 30 | 31 | ✓

f)

| 78 | 79 | 80 | ✓

6 marks

3  Use the < or > symbols correctly for these numbers.

a) 14 < 16 ✓

b) 76 > 56 ✓

c) 23 < 25 √

d) 89 > 34 √

e) 67 > 66 ✓

f) 88 < 99 ✓

6 marks

4  Fill in the correct symbol to make these calculations correct.

a) 4 – 3 = 1 √

b) 14 + 6 = 20 √

c) 23 – 7 = 16 √

d) 9 – 9 = 0 √

4 marks

5  How many two-digit numbers can you make from the single-digit numbers 2, 4 and 6? Write them in the spaces below.

24    26    42    46    62    64

6 marks

# What is a Fraction?

- Recognise, find and name a half as one of two equal parts of an object, shape or quantity
- Recognise, find and name a quarter as one of four equal parts of an object, shape or quantity

## Understanding Fractions

A **fraction** is part of a **whole** object, group of objects or a number. A fraction is made up of two numbers – a **numerator** at the top and a **denominator** at the bottom.

## Key Point

The bottom number of a fraction always says how many equal parts make a whole.

## Halves

A **half** ($\frac{1}{2}$) is a fraction:

The top number (numerator) tells you how many parts of the whole you have.

$$\frac{1}{2}$$

The bottom number (denominator) tells you how many equal parts are in the whole.

## Tip

Remember that the 'd' in denominator means it is the 'down' part of the fraction.

A half ($\frac{1}{2}$) of this circle is shaded:

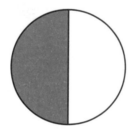

### Example

Look at the block. The block as a whole would be $\frac{2}{2}$.

- This means that two of the possible two parts are there.
- The blue fraction of the block would be $\frac{1}{2}$ of the whole.
- The pink fraction would also be $\frac{1}{2}$ of the whole block.

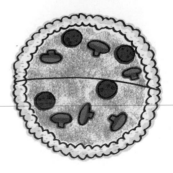

# Quarters

A quarter fraction is shown by $\frac{1}{4}$. The numerator (top number) is telling you that one part is shown and the denominator (bottom number) tells you that four equal parts make up the whole.

### Example

This flag shows one-quarter ($\frac{1}{4}$) coloured red. What fraction of the flag is not coloured?

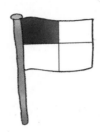

If four parts make up the whole and only one part is coloured, then there must be three parts that are not coloured. This means that $\frac{3}{4}$ of the flag is not coloured.

# Ordering Fractions and Whole Numbers

Fractions can be shown on a number line. Look at this example.

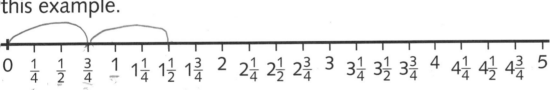

$$0 \quad \frac{1}{4} \quad \frac{1}{2} \quad \frac{3}{4} \quad 1 \quad 1\frac{1}{4} \quad 1\frac{1}{2} \quad 1\frac{3}{4} \quad 2 \quad 2\frac{1}{4} \quad 2\frac{1}{2} \quad 2\frac{3}{4} \quad 3 \quad 3\frac{1}{4} \quad 3\frac{1}{2} \quad 3\frac{3}{4} \quad 4 \quad 4\frac{1}{4} \quad 4\frac{1}{2} \quad 4\frac{3}{4} \quad 5$$

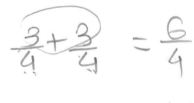

$$\frac{3}{4} + \frac{3}{4} = \frac{6}{4}$$

### Quick Test

1. Write the fractions alongside each circle to show the dark green parts. $\frac{1}{4}$     $\frac{3}{4}$

   a) 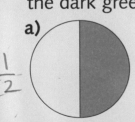    b) 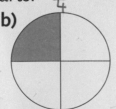    c)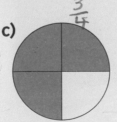

   $\frac{1}{2}$

2. Write the symbol for a half. $\frac{1}{2}$
3. What is $\frac{4}{4}$ the same as? 1 whole

### Key Words

- Fraction
- Whole
- Numerator
- Denominator
- Half

29

# Halves and Quarters

- Recognise the equivalence of $\frac{2}{4}$ and $\frac{1}{2}$
- Work out simple fractions, for example $\frac{1}{2}$ of 6 = 3

## Combining Halves and Quarters

Halves and quarters can be combined.

Look at the circle. It is split into quarters. Can you see that two-quarters make up half of the circle?

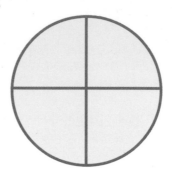

This means that two-quarters is equal to one-half. This is known as an **equivalent** fraction.

> **Key Point**
>
> A half is the same as two-quarters. It is an equivalent fraction.

### Example

Look at the square:

- $\frac{3}{4}$ is coloured
- $\frac{2}{4}$ is the same colour (yellow)
- the final quarter is a different colour (blue).

This means that half of the square is one colour and a quarter is a different colour.

But altogether $\frac{3}{4}$ of the whole square is coloured.

> **Key Point**
>
> A fraction is always an equal part of something.

## Finding a Fraction of a Group

You can discover a fraction of a **group**.

### Example 1

Look at the four lemons. If you think of them as a group, then two lemons would be half of the group.

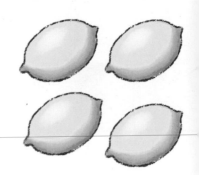

How many lemons would a quarter be? 1 ✓

A quarter of the group would be one lemon.

## Example 2

There are four worms in a group. How many worms would be $\frac{3}{4}$ of the group?

If four worms make the full group, each worm is worth $\frac{1}{4}$ of the whole.

So, $\frac{3}{4}$ of the group would be three worms.

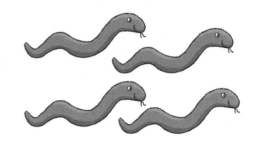

## Quick Test

1. Colour $\frac{1}{2}$ of each shape.

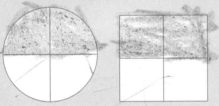

2. Colour $\frac{1}{4}$ of each shape.

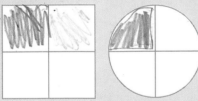

3. Colour $\frac{3}{4}$ of each shape.

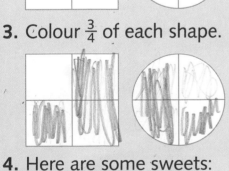

4. Here are some sweets:

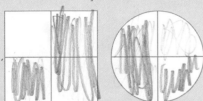

a) How many sweets equal $\frac{1}{4}$ of the group?

b) How many sweets equal $\frac{1}{2}$ of the group?

### Key Words

- Equivalent
- Group

# Finding Fractions of Larger Groups

- Recognise and find fractions of groups and numbers

## How Do You Find a Fraction of a Group of More Than Four?

You can find a fraction of a group of more than four by dividing by 2. **Even** numbers can always be **halved** equally but not always **quartered** (for example 14 cannot be quartered).

If half of a group of 4 is 2, then what would half of a group of 8 be? 4

If you divide the group in half, then there are two equal groups of four snakes. This means that half of the whole group is four snakes.

A quarter of the group would be two snakes.

### Example

Beth has six strawberries.

Beth's friend wants half of them. Count all of the strawberries in the group and divide that number by 2 to find half:

$6 \div 2 = 3$

Beth's friend would get three strawberries because this is half of the group.

> **Tip**
>
> Find half of a number by dividing it into two equal parts.

> **Key Point**
>
> Odd numbers in a group cannot be halved equally into whole numbers.

# Fractions of a Number

If you can find a fraction of a group of objects, then you can find a fraction of a number.

## Example

This number is 12. If you divide 12 by 2 to get two equal amounts, then the answer is 6:

$12 \div 2 = 6 \qquad 6 + 6 = 12$

So half of 12 must be 6.

To find a quarter of 12 you need to halve the 6:

$6 \div 2 = 3 \qquad 3 + 3 = 6$

So a quarter of 12 is 3.

Check this by splitting 12 into four equal parts:

$3 + 3 + 3 + 3 = 12$

A quarter of 12 is 3.

If you divide 12 by 3, you can find a third ($\frac{1}{3}$):

$12 \div 3 = 4$

A third of 12 is 4.

## Tip

Finding a quarter of a larger group is like dividing the whole number of the group by 2 and dividing that number by 2 again to find a quarter.

## Quick Test

**1.** What would half of this number be? *8*

# 16

**2.** Find $\frac{1}{4}$ of this number. *4*
**3.** What would three-quarters of this number be? *12*
**4.** Find $\frac{2}{4}$ of this number. *8*

## Key Words

• Even
• Halved
• Quartered

33

# Practice Questions

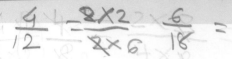

$\frac{4}{12} = \frac{2 \times 2}{2 \times 6} = \frac{6}{18}$  $=$  $\frac{8}{24}$

**1** Look at the blocks.

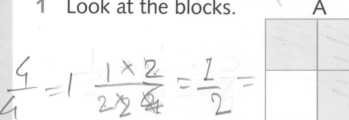

$\frac{4}{4} = 1$ $\frac{1 \times 2}{2 \times 2 \times 4} = \frac{1}{2} =$

A       B       C

a) Which block shows the fraction $\frac{1}{2}$?  _____C_____  ☐ 1 mark

b) Which block has three-quarters coloured?  _____A_____  ☐ 1 mark

c) One of the blocks has $\frac{1}{4}$ coloured.
   Which one is it?  _____B_____  ☐ 1 mark

**1** Write down the fraction that shows four equal
   parts making the whole.  ☐ 1 mark

**2** Add the fractions: $\frac{1}{2} + \frac{1}{4} =$    ☐ 1 mark

$\frac{4}{4}$
$\frac{2}{6}$
$\frac{1}{2}$
$\frac{1}{2}$

**3** Which is the larger fraction: $\frac{1}{4}$ or $\frac{1}{2}$?  ☐ 1 mark

**4** Which fraction is equivalent to $\frac{2}{4}$?  ☐ 1 mark

**1** Look at the ants.

a) How many ants equal half of the whole group?  ____4____  ☐ 1 mark

b) A quarter of the group would be ____2____ ants.  ☐ 1 mark

c) Six ants would be $\boxed{\frac{3}{4}}$ of the group.  ☐ 1 mark

## Review Questions

1   Answer the following multiplication problems.

   a) $5 \times 2$  = _____ 10 _____   ☐ 1 mark

   b) $2 \times 5$  = _____ 10 _____   ☐ 1 mark

   c) $5 \times 10$ = _____ 50 _____   ☐ 1 mark

S  2   Look at the groups of sweets. Write the multiplication that describes the groups.

_____ $3 \times 2 = 6$ _____   ☐ 1 mark

3   Find the answers to these division problems.

   a) $8 \div 2$  = _____ 4 _____   ☐ 1 mark

   b) $15 \div 5$ = _____ 3 _____   ☐ 1 mark

   c) $20 \div 2$ = _____ 10 _____   ☐ 1 mark

4   What is the inverse of $3 \times 2 = 6$? _____ $6 \div 3 = 2$ _____   ☐ 1 mark

5   Check this division calculation by using the inverse multiplication sum.

   $\boxed{10} \div \boxed{2} = \boxed{5}$ _____ $5 \times 2 = 10$ _____   ☐ 1 mark

6   Double these numbers.

   a) $\boxed{5}$  _____ 10 _____   ☐ 1 mark

   b) $\boxed{10}$ _____ 20 _____   ☐ 1 mark

   c) $\boxed{12}$ _____ 24 _____   ☐ 1 mark

7   Halve these numbers.

   a) $\boxed{6}$  _____ 3 _____   ☐ 1 mark

   b) $\boxed{14}$ _____ 7 _____   ☐ 1 mark

   c) $\boxed{16}$ _____ 8 _____   ☐ 1 mark

# Standard Units of Measure

- Choose and use standard units of measure for length, mass and capacity
- Compare and order length, mass and capacity using the correct symbols

## What are Standard Units of Measure?

Standard units of measure are ways of measuring that are the same for everyone.

Standard measurements are used for **length**, **weight**, temperature and **capacity**.

## Measuring Length

The standard unit used to measure length is **centimetres** (cm).

100 cm is equal to 1 **metre** (1 m).

### Example

The first pencil measures 3 cm. The second is 2 cm and is the shortest pencil. The third pencil is 4 cm in length and is the longest of them all.

## Measuring Mass

The **mass** of something is its weight. Mass is measured in **grams** (g) and **kilograms** (kg). There are 1000 g in 1 kg.

> **Key Point**
>
> 1 kilogram (1 kg) is made up of 1000 grams (1000 g).

## Example

The first scale shows that the bananas weigh 1.5 kg or 1500 g. The second scale shows that the shoe weighs 400 g. The bananas are heavier than the shoe.

**Tip**

'Kilo-' means one thousand.

Both these scales are measuring in kilograms (kg). Each smaller mark equals 100 grams (g).

# Measuring Capacity

The capacity of something is how much it contains. Capacity is measured in **litres** (l) and **millilitres** (ml). There are 1000 millilitres in 1 litre.

## Example

**Tip**

Remember to include the unit in which you are measuring (cm, m, g, kg, ml, l).

Both these jugs hold the same capacity, but each contains a different amount. Each longer mark represents 100 ml.

- The first jug is full and contains 1 litre.
- The second jug contains 400 ml.

500ml   500ml   500ml   500ml

## Quick Test

1. What is the mass of the book? __500__ g
2. How much water is in the jug? __600__ ml
3. What length is the blue line? __4__ cm

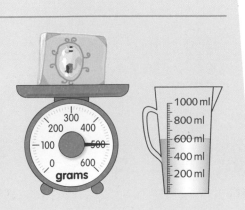

**Key Words**

- Length
- Weight
- Capacity
- Centimetre
- Metre
- Mass
- Gram
- Kilogram
- Litre
- Millilitre

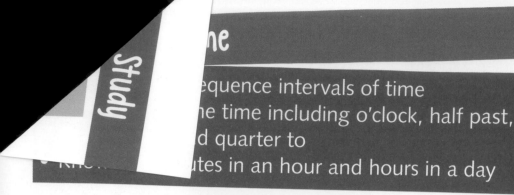

Study

equence intervals of time

he time including o'clock, half past,
d quarter to

tes in an hour and hours in a day

# How is Time Measured?

Time is measured using a standard unit. Smaller amounts of time are measured in **seconds**, **minutes** and **hours**. Larger units of time are measured in days, weeks, months and years.

| 60 seconds = 1 minute |
|---|
| 60 minutes = 1 hour |
| 24 hours = 1 day |
| 7 days = 1 week |
| 52 weeks = 1 year |
| 12 months = 1 year |

A clock is used to measure the smaller units of time. This clock is set at 2 **o'clock**.

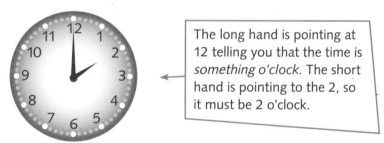

The long hand is pointing at 12 telling you that the time is *something o'clock*. The short hand is pointing to the 2, so it must be 2 o'clock.

### Example

A   B   C

Clock A shows a time of **half past** two. The long hand has gone half way around the clock so the time is half past two.

**Key Point**

It is always *something past the hour* until the long hand goes past the 6. It then becomes *something to the hour.*

O'clock

**Key Point**

Each number on a clock represents a five-minute interval.

**Tip**

You can measure time in fractions of an hour.

38

When the long hand is pointing at the number 3, it has gone a quarter of the way around the clock. Clock B shows **quarter past** one.

If the long hand points to the 9, it is **quarter to**. Clock C shows quarter to four.

# Days and Months

These are the days of the week:

Monday    Wednesday    Friday    Sunday
Tuesday    Thursday    Saturday

These are the months of the year:

January    March    May    July    September    November
February    April    June    August    October    December

## Quick Test

**1.** Draw hands on the clocks to show the time in quarter of an hour intervals starting at 4 o'clock.

**2.** Today is Wednesday, so what day is tomorrow? Thursday

**3.** Name the rest of the months in order:
January, February, March

### Key Words

- Second
- Minute
- Hour
- O'clock
- Half past
- Quarter past
- Quarter to

# Standard Units of Money

- Recognise and use symbols for pounds (£) and pence (p)
- Combine amounts to make a particular value
- Solve simple problems including giving change

## Standard Units of Money

In the UK the standard units of money are **pounds** (£) and **pence** (p). Other countries sometimes use different standard units of money.

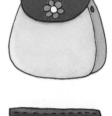

Units of money are known as **currency**.

Pounds can be **coins** or **notes** depending on their value. Pence are coins that are worth different amounts.

Here are some of the coins and notes used as standard currency in the UK:

Coins can be used in different **combinations** to make the same amount.

> **Key Point**
>
> 100 pence equals 1 pound (or 100p equals £1).

### Example

Look at the coins. Each group has the same value but uses a different combination of coins.

The total value of each group is 5p.

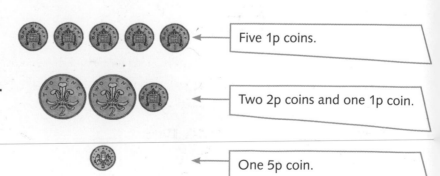

Five 1p coins.

Two 2p coins and one 1p coin.

One 5p coin.

# Giving Change

If you buy something and you pay with too much money, you will be given some money back as change.

### Example

Joshua wanted to buy a banana costing 17p.
He gave the shopkeeper 20p.

The shopkeeper gave Joshua 3p change.

20p – 17p = 3p

**Key Point**

When you pay with too much money, you will get some money back. This is called change.

## Quick Test

1.

   Using different numbers of the coins above, write down six different combinations you could use to make a total of 10p.

   < 2p + 2p + 2p + 2p + 2p

   5p + 5p

   1p + 1p + 1p + 1p + 1p + 1p + 1p + 1p + 1p + 1p

   10p + 0p

   2p + 2p + 5p + 1p

   2p + 5p + 1p + 1p + 1p

   2 + 5 + 1 + 2

2. Item 1          Item 2          Item 3

   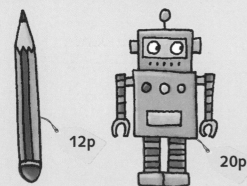

   12p          20p           16p

   If you had a 20p coin, how much change would you receive if you bought each of the items separately?
   a) Item 1: _____8_____ p change
   b) Item 2: _____0_____ p change
   c) Item 3: _____4_____ p change

**Key Words**

- Pounds
- Pence
- Currency
- Coin
- Note
- Combination

# Practice Questions

PS Problem-solving questions

1 Put these ribbons in order of length from shortest to longest.

*B, C, A*

1 mark

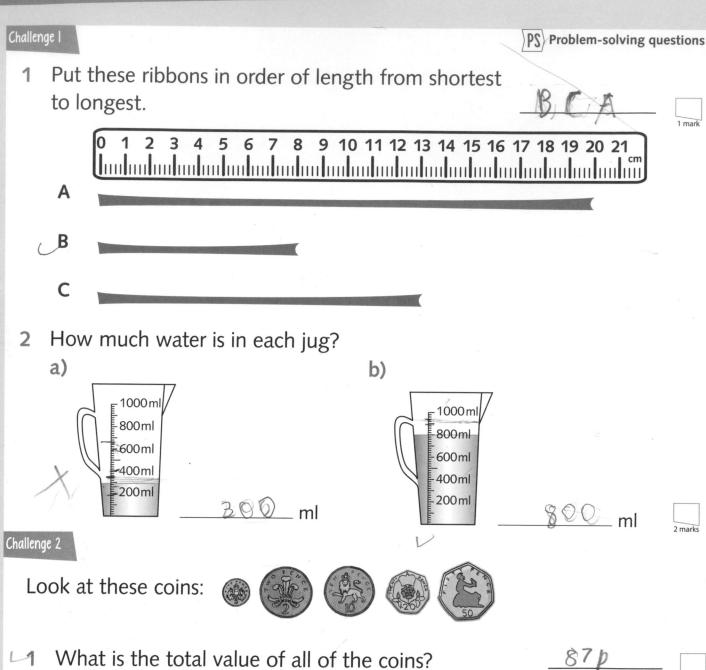

2 How much water is in each jug?

a)

*300* ml

b)

*800* ml

2 marks

Challenge 2

Look at these coins:

1 What is the total value of all of the coins? _____ *87p*

1 mark

PS 2 How much more money would you need to have £1? _____ *13p*

1 mark

Challenge 3

Look at this clock and write your answers in words:

PS 1 What will the time be in one hour? _____ *quater past three*

1 mark

PS 2 What will the time be in half an hour? _____ *quater post 2*

1 mark

# Review Questions

PS Problem-solving questions

**1** Write the fraction coloured in each of these shapes.

a) $\dfrac{1}{2}$     V     b) $\dfrac{1}{4}$     c) $\dfrac{3}{4}$

3 marks

**2** How many halves are there in $2\frac{1}{2}$?

5

1 mark

**3** How many quarters are there in $1\frac{3}{4}$?

7

$\dfrac{1}{2}$   1   $1\frac{?}{4}$   2   2

1 mark

**4** Starting at $\frac{3}{4}$ and counting on $\frac{1}{2}$ what number do you arrive at?

$1\frac{1}{4}$

$\dfrac{3}{4} + \dfrac{1}{2}$

1 mark

**5** How many quarters are there to reach number 2?

8

$\frac{3}{4}$   $1\frac{1}{4}$   $1\frac{1}{2}$   $1\,3/4$

1 mark

**6** Count back three-quarters from number 3. Where do you finish?

$2\frac{1}{4}$

$2\frac{1}{4}$   $2\frac{2}{4}$   $2\frac{3}{4}$   3

1 mark

PS **7** Look at this group of caterpillars:

a) How many would half of this group of caterpillars be?

4

1 mark

b) What would a quarter of the group be?    2

1 mark

**8** What is half of 16?    8

1 mark

## 2-D and 3-D Shapes

- Recognise and name common 2-D and 3-D shapes
- Name simple properties of 2-D and 3-D shapes

# 2-D Shapes

A **2-D shape** is sometimes called a **flat shape**. Here are the most common 2-D shapes.

circle    triangle    square    rectangle    pentagon    hexagon

If you look at each of them, they all have different **properties**. Properties are special features of that **shape** that allow it to be described.

### Example

- The triangle has three straight sides and three **corners**.

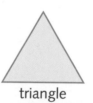

triangle

- The square has different properties. A square has four straight sides that are all equal in length. It has four corners.

square

**Key Point**

Not all triangles look the same, but they are still triangles.

# 3-D Shapes

A **3-D shape** is also known as a **solid** shape. Here are the most common 3-D shapes.

  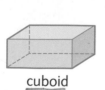   

sphere    cube    cuboid    cone    triangular-based pyramid    cylinder

**Tip**

Remember to include the faces that you can't see in a drawing of a 3-D shape.

3-D shapes also have their own properties that help you to identify them.

## Example

- A cube has six faces that are equal and square. It has 12 straight **edges** and eight **vertices**.

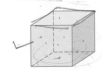

cube

- A cuboid also has six faces. It also has 12 straight edges and eight vertices.

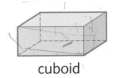

cuboid

A cuboid has some rectangular faces, which make it different to a cube. All six faces of a cuboid can be rectangular or the two end faces may be squares.

## Quick Test

1. What 2-D shape is described here?  _rectangle_

   This shape has four straight sides and four corners. It has two short sides and two long sides.

rectangle

2. Give two properties of a square-based pyramid.

_5 corners_
_8 edges_

square-based pyramid

_5 vertices_
_9 edges_

3. Which of these 3-D shapes has no corners or flat faces?

 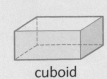   _sphere_

   cylinder        cuboid         sphere

4. A pentagon has five straight sides. Which of these shapes is a pentagon?

A    B    C    D    E    F

**Key Words**

- 2-D shape
- Flat shape
- Properties
- Shape
- Corner
- 3-D shape
- Solid
- Face
- Edge
- Vertex (vertices)

## Different Shapes

- Compare and sort common 2-D and 3-D shapes and everyday objects
- Understand what symmetry is

# Different Shapes

Some 2-D and 3-D shapes may look different in appearance but they are still the same kind of shape.

Triangles, rectangles, cylinders, cuboids and pyramids come in many different forms but they still share the same properties with other shapes of the same kind.

Look at these 3-D shapes. They are all different but all three are cylinders.

Sometimes all the sides and all the angles of a 2-D shape are equal. Then the shape is **regular**.

> **Key Point**
>
> Some shapes look different to each other but still have the properties of that shape.

# Everyday Objects

2-D and 3-D shapes are used for everyday objects.

> **Tip**
>
> Look for examples of 3-D shapes around your house.

**Example**

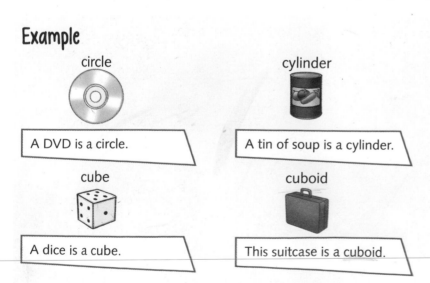

circle

A DVD is a circle.

cylinder

A tin of soup is a cylinder.

cube

A dice is a cube.

cuboid

This suitcase is a cuboid.

# Symmetry

**Symmetry** means a shape is the same on each side when a line is drawn through the middle of it.

If a shape is **symmetrical**, then it is the same on both sides.

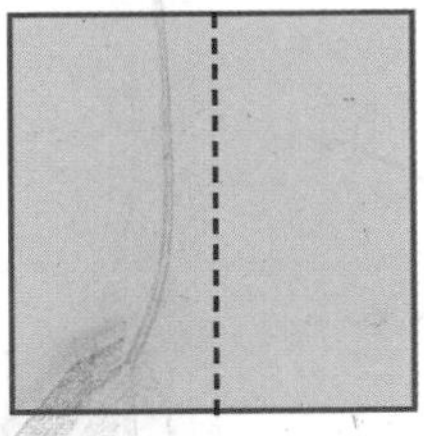

This square is divided into two equal parts by a line of symmetry.

A square has other lines of symmetry too:

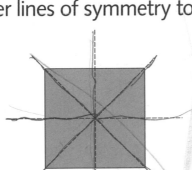

**Key Point**

A line of symmetry can go up and down, across or diagonally.

## Quick Test

1. Match the description to the shape. Write the correct letter on the shape.

   **a)** This shape has six faces and eight vertices.

   **b)** This shape has three straight sides.

   **c)** This shape has five straight sides.

   **d)** This shape has two faces that are circles.

   **e)** This shape has six straight sides.

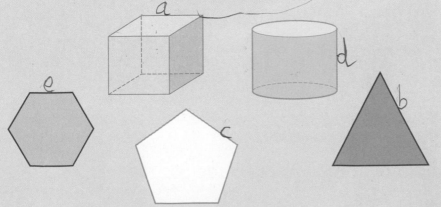

2. Name one item that is cylinder-shaped.

**Key Words**

- Regular
- Symmetry
- Symmetrical

# Practice Questions

## Challenge 1

**PS** Problem-solving questions

1 Name these 2-D shapes.

a) pentagon b) circle c) rectangle

3 marks

2 A 2-D shape has six straight sides. The shape is a hexagon.

1 mark

## Challenge 2

1 Name these 3-D shapes.

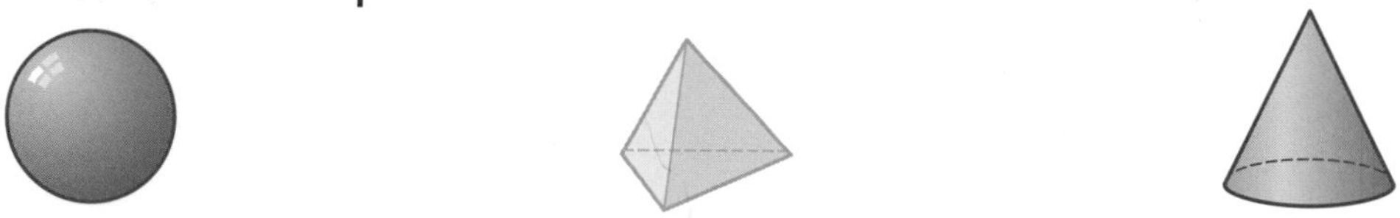

a) sphere b) piramid c) cone

3 marks

2 Write down two properties of a cuboid.

8 vertices 6 faces

2 marks

**PS** 3 This 3-D shape has no straight edges and two of its faces are circles.

The shape is a cylinder.

1 mark

## Challenge 3

1 Draw a line of symmetry on each of these 2-D shapes.

2 marks

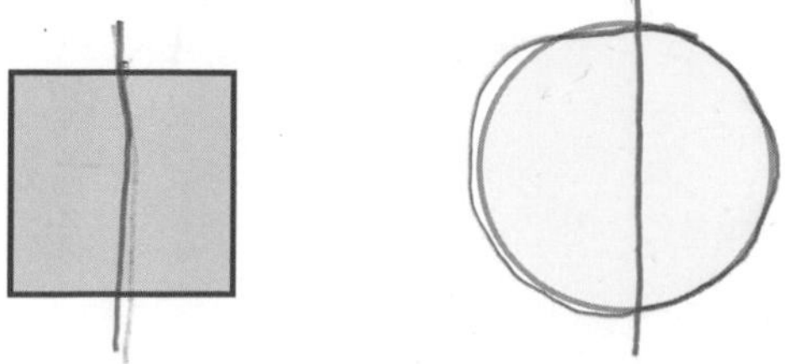

2 Put an X on all of the vertices that you can see.

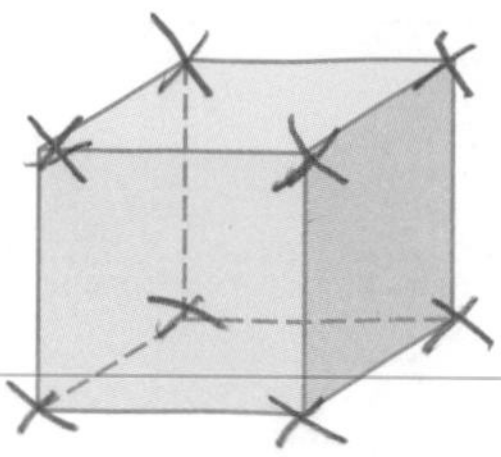

8 marks

# Review Questions

PS Problem-solving questions

PS 1 Look at the worms.

A

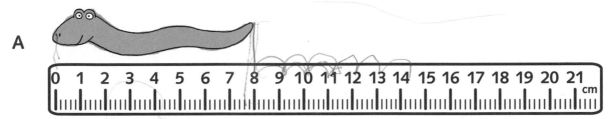

B

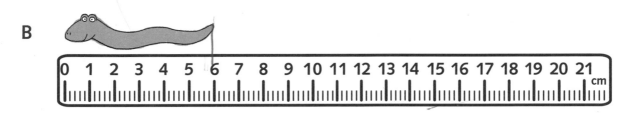

a) What is the length of each worm?

i) A = 8 cm  ii) B = 6 cm  2 marks

b) If both worms were joined together, how long would they be?

14 cm  1 mark

PS 2 Look at the cylinders.

A

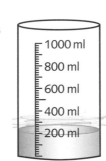

B

a) How much water is in each cylinder? 200ml  1 mark

b) What is the total amount of water in both cylinders?

400ml  1 mark

PS 3 What time (in words) would it be in one hour?

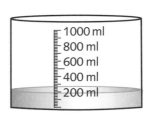

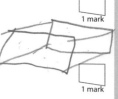

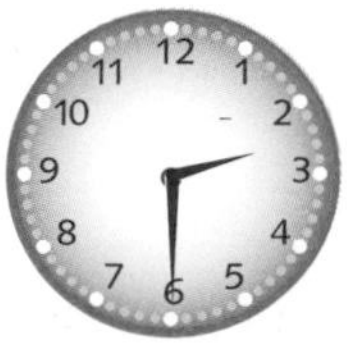

half past three  1 mark

4 What is the total value of the coins?

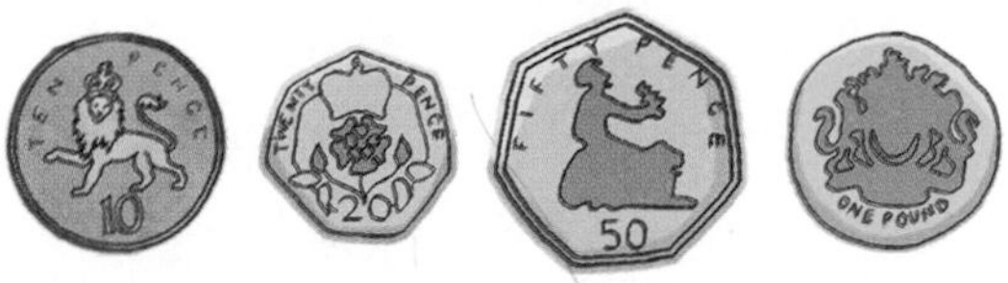

£1.80  1 mark

## Patterns and Sequences

- Order and arrange combinations of mathematical objects in patterns and sequences
- Use mathematical vocabulary, such as above and below, to describe position, direction and movement

# What is a Pattern or Sequence?

A **pattern** or sequence is when the order of something is **repeated**.

Patterns and sequences can appear in lots of different ways.

> **Key Point**
>
> A pattern or sequence has an order that repeats.

### Example

Look at the squares. Can you see a repeating pattern of colours?

The first three squares are blue. They are followed by one orange square and then the sequence repeats.

So the next three squares will be blue.

# Patterns and Sequences of Numbers

Numbers can also form patterns and sequences.

### Example

1, 1, 2, 2, 3, 3, 4, 4 is a repeating sequence.

If you look at the sequence, each number is repeated twice.

So that means that 5, 5 would be next in the sequence.

> **Tip**
>
> You need to look at the whole pattern or sequence, not just the start of it, to work out what comes next.

# Directions and Movement

A **direction** is the way something is moving. If you change direction, then you have altered where you are going.

To change direction you have to turn.

### Example

Look at the clocks. The arrow around the first clock shows the hands moving in   a **clockwise** direction. The arrow around the second clock shows the hands moving in an **anti-clockwise** direction. A clockwise turn is to the right. An anti-clockwise turn is to the left.

Look at the picture of the star, planet and spaceship. You could use the words **top**, **middle** and **bottom** to describe their positions. You could also say the star is above the planet and the spaceship is below the planet.

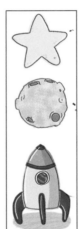

Here the star is at the top. The planet is in the middle. The spaceship is at the bottom.

## Quick Test

1. What are the next four triangles in this sequence?

2. If you stood on the X facing the carrot, which direction would you turn to face the apple if you wanted to make the shortest turn? Clockwise or anti-clockwise? *clockwise*

# Turns

- Understand rotation and describe turns
- Understand half turns and quarter turns
- Follow directions and describe movement in a straight line

## Fractions of a Turn

The amount that you turn can be measured in fractions of a turn. A **quarter turn** is also called a **right-angle turn**. There is also a **three-quarter turn**.

Another word for a turn is **rotation**.

### Example

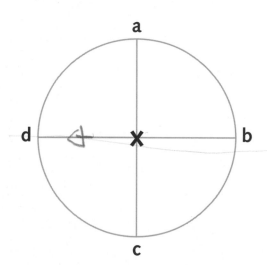

Imagine that you were standing on the **X** at the centre of this circle. You are facing **a** and want to face **b**. You would make a quarter, or right-angle turn, clockwise, in order to face **b**.

To return to **a** you would need to make an anti-clockwise, quarter turn.

If you were facing **a** and wanted to turn to face **c**, then you could make a **half turn** clockwise or anti-clockwise.

# Following Directions

To follow directions you need to understand the instructions or you might end up in the wrong place!

### Example

Look at the map and follow these directions.

**1.** Place a finger on 'START' and move forward five squares heading past the trees.

**2.** Make a quarter turn clockwise.

**3.** Move forward one square.

You should now be at the square containing the key!

**Tip**

Remember – a clockwise turn is a right turn.

### Quick Test

**1.** Use the grid above to write a list of seven directions to collect the coin and get to the house. You **cannot** move through squares that have trees.
Good luck!

Begin at the square that has the key, facing in the direction you finished in step 3 above.

**Key Words**

- Quarter turn
- Right-angle turn
- Three-quarter turn
- Rotation
- Half turn

53

Challenge 1

1 Look at the pattern of triangles.

The next two triangles will be ___yellow___ and ___green___.

1 mark

PS 2 Look at this sequence and fill in the missing numbers.

2 2 2, 4 4 4, ___66 6___, 8 8 8, ___10 10 10___, 12 12 12

2 marks

3 Is a left turn clockwise or anti-clockwise?___anti-clockwise___

1 mark

Challenge 2

1 If you were standing at X looking at number 1, would you move clockwise or anti-clockwise to face number 4 in the shortest turn?

___anti - clockwise___

1 mark

2 What kind of turn would you make in question 1? Tick the correct answer.

a) A quarter turn clockwise. ☐

b) A quarter turn anti-clockwise. ✓

c) A half turn anti-clockwise. ☐

1 mark

Challenge 3

PS 1 Continue this sequence.

9–8, 1–2, 7–6, 3–4, ___5–4___, ___5–6___ ? 3-2, 7-8

2 marks

2 Describe this number pattern. 2, 5, 8, 11, 14

_____

1 mark

PS 3 You take two steps forwards, turn right and take three steps, then turn to the left and make five steps.

How many steps have you made in total? ___10___

1 mark

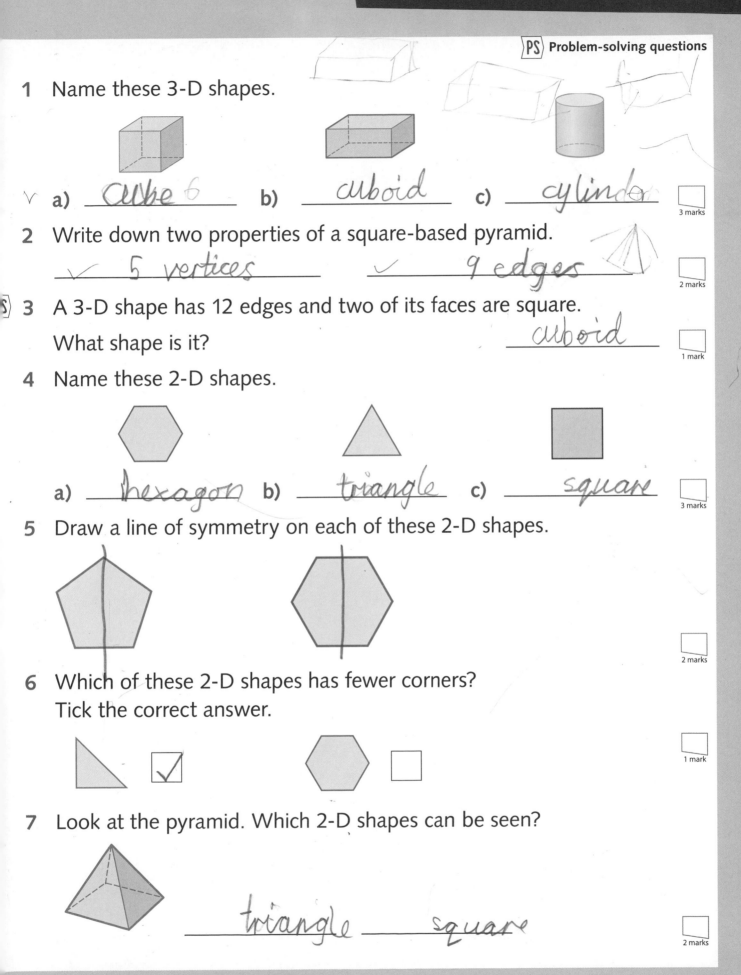

PS Problem-solving questions

1   Name these 3-D shapes.

✓ a) ___Cube 6___   b) ___cuboid___   c) ___cylinder___   ☐ 3 marks

2   Write down two properties of a square-based pyramid.

✓ ___5 vertices___   ✓ ___9 edges___   ☐ 2 marks

3   A 3-D shape has 12 edges and two of its faces are square.
    What shape is it?   ___cuboid___   ☐ 1 mark

4   Name these 2-D shapes.

a) ___hexagon___   b) ___triangle___   c) ___square___   ☐ 3 marks

5   Draw a line of symmetry on each of these 2-D shapes.

☐ 2 marks

6   Which of these 2-D shapes has fewer corners?
    Tick the correct answer.

☑   ☐   ☐ 1 mark

7   Look at the pyramid. Which 2-D shapes can be seen?

___triangle___   ___square___   ☐ 2 marks

55

# Pictograms, Charts and Graphs

- Interpret and construct simple pictograms, tally charts and block diagrams
- Answer simple questions by counting the number of objects in each category and sorting them by quantity

## What is a Pictogram?

A **pictogram** is a way of showing **information** using pictures.

### Example

Look at this pictogram. It shows information about snacks brought into school.

The pictogram shows that three children brought an apple, because there are three apples.

How many children brought grapes? 4

If you count the bunches of grapes, there are four. So four children brought grapes.

Key:  = 1 child brought an apple

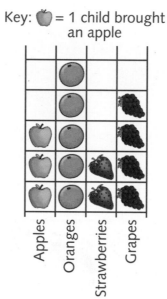

**Key Point**

The category with the biggest number is the most popular. The category with the smallest number is the least popular.

## Tally Charts

A **tally chart** is used to show data. A tally chart counts in lots of five.

A vertical mark shows one object up to four objects. The fifth object is marked by a diagonal line. So this tally shows 8.

**Key Point**

A tally chart counts in lots of five.

### Example

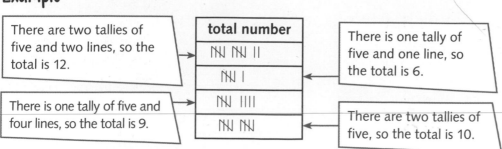

There are two tallies of five and two lines, so the total is 12.

There is one tally of five and four lines, so the total is 9.

| total number |
|---|
| ⵜⵜ ⵜⵜ II |
| ⵜⵜ I |
| ⵜⵜ IIII |
| ⵜⵜ ⵜⵜ |

There is one tally of five and one line, so the total is 6.

There are two tallies of five, so the total is 10.

# Block Graphs

**Block graphs** show information using a number **scale**. They are better at showing larger amounts.

### Example

Look at the graph about snails. If you use the number scale at the side, you can see how many snails were found. The scale counts in lots of five.

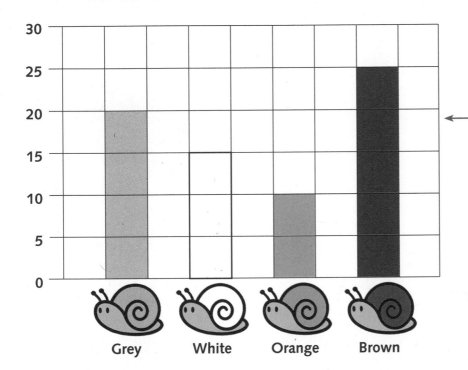

The scale tells you that 20 grey snails, 15 white snails, 10 orange snails and 25 brown snails were found.

### Quick Test

1. Use the block graph above to answer these questions.
   a) What was the most common snail? *brown snail*
   b) What was the total of grey and white snails? *35*
   c) Fill in this tally chart to represent the information shown in the block graph.

| Coloured snail | Tally |
|---|---|
| Grey | *20* |
| White | *15* |
| Orange | *10* |
| Brown | *25* |

### Key Words

- Pictogram
- Information
- Tally chart
- Block graph
- Scale

# Gathering Information and Using Data

## What is Data?

**Data** is information. You can share data by making a **graph**, **table** or **chart** to display it.

You can also make a graph of someone else's data.

### Example

Look at this tally chart. It shows a tally of favourite pets.

| | | |
|---|---|---|
| **Rabbit** | 🐰 | IIII |
| **Dog** | 🐕 | NN I |
| **Cat** | 🐈 | NN III |
| **Fish** | 🐟 | NN |

If you were to use the data from the chart to make a block graph, it would be easier to understand.

To construct a block graph, you need to write the numbers (amounts) on the vertical axis and the pets on the horizontal axis.

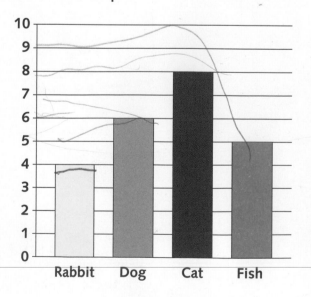

# Interpreting Data

You need to be able to interpret data shown in tables and charts.

## Example

Children at a school collected information about the weather in May. They marked each school day with a symbol to show what the weather was like.

**Weather in May**

| | Day 1 | Day 2 | Day 3 | Day 4 | Day 5 |
|---|---|---|---|---|---|
| **Week 1** | ☔ | ☔ | ☔ | ☀ | ☀ |
| **Week 2** | ☀ | ☁ | ☁ | ☁ | ☔ |
| **Week 3** | ☀ | ☀ | ☀ | ☀ | ☁ |
| **Week 4** | ☔ | ☔ | ☔ | ☔ | ☔ |

> During the first week it was sunny for two days but it rained for three days.

**Tip**

Remember that data is just another word for information.

When you collect information over a period of time and arrange it that way, it is called **chronological**.

## Quick Test

1. Use the 'Weather in May' table to help you answer these questions.
   a) How many days was it cloudy but dry? 4
   b) How many days did it rain? 8
   c) It was sunny for _____7_____ days.
   d) Over how many days did the children gather information? 20 days

**Key Words**

- Data
- Graph
- Table
- Chart
- Chronological

# Practice Questions

PS Problem-solving questions

1   Make a tally of these sweets.

| Sweets | Tally |
|---|---|
| | ʈʜʟʟ ʈʜʟʟ ʈʜ ∥∥ |
| | ʈʜʟʟ ∥∥∥ |
| | ∥∥∖ |

3 marks

PS 1   Look at the table showing children's hair colour in a class.

| Blonde | |
|---|---|
| Brown | |
| Black | |

Key:
= 1 child

a)  How many children had blonde hair?  _____5_____

1 mark

b)  There are _____2_____ more children with brown hair than black.

1 mark

c)  What is the total of children shown?  _____15_____

1 mark

1   Look at the block graph.

a)  How many minutes does it take to bake a bread cake?

_____7_____

b)  How many minutes does a small loaf take to bake?

_____12_____

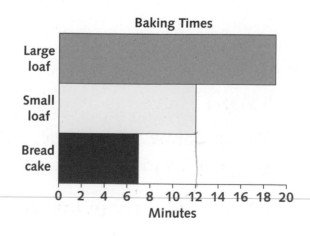

Baking Times

2 marks

1 Look at this collection of things.

a) What is above the ball? _____apple_____ ☐ 1 mark

b) What is next to the beaker? teddy bear_____ ☐ 1 mark

c) Which two things are below the ball?
   ___sandwich___  ___beaker___ ☐ 1 mark

d) What is to the left of the ball? banana _____ ☐ 1 mark

2 Find your way through the maze
using clockwise (right) and anti-clockwise
(left) turns.

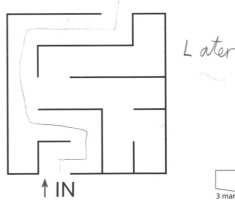

Later

a) Draw your route through the maze.

b) Circle clockwise turns in green.

c) Circle anti-clockwise turns in red.

↑ IN

☐ 3 marks

3 Draw the shapes in the correct position in the grid.

a) A triangle is in the **centre** square.

b) A star is **above** the triangle.

c) An X is **below** the triangle.

d) A circle is to the **left** of the triangle.

e) A Y is to the **right** of the star.

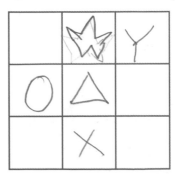

☐ 5 marks

**PS** 1   Jai made a tally chart showing the colour of cars passing school.

| Car | Tally |
|-----|-------|
| Red | ⵏⵏⵏ ⵏⵏⵏ ⵏⵏⵏ II |
| Black | ⵏⵏⵏ ⵏⵏⵏ II |
| Blue | ⵏⵏⵏ II |

a)   How many black cars passed school?    _12_    ☐ 1 mark

b)   How many red cars passed school?    _17_    ☐ 1 mark

c)   What was the total number of cars?    _36_    ☐ 1 mark

2   Beth counted the birds visiting her feeders. She counted 8 blackbirds, 3 robins and 11 sparrows.

Show this information as a tally chart.

| Bird | Tally |
|------|-------|
| Blackbird | ⵏⵏⵏ III |
| Robin | III |
| Sparrow | ⵏⵏⵏ ⵏⵏⵏ I |

☐ 3 marks

**PS** 3   Use the chart to answer these questions.

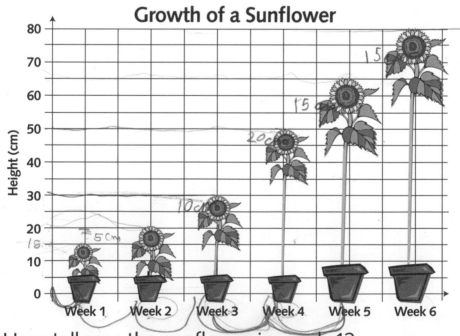

Growth of a Sunflower

a)   How tall was the sunflower in week 1?    _115_    ☐ 1 mark

b)   How tall was the sunflower in week 3?    _30 cm_    ☐ 1 mark

c)   Between which two weeks did the sunflower grow the most?

_Week 3_    ☐ 1 mark

PS Problem-solving questions

PS **1** Look at these biscuits:

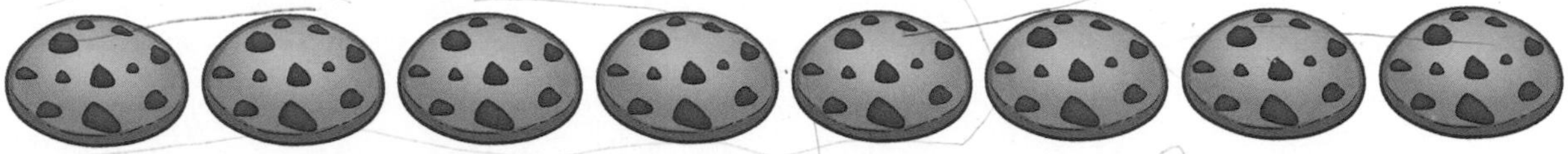

**a)** How many biscuits equal $\frac{1}{4}$ of the group? 2 ________ (1 mark)

**b)** How many biscuits equal $\frac{1}{2}$ of the group? 4 ________ (1 mark)

**c)** How many biscuits equal $\frac{3}{4}$ of the group? 6 ________ (1 mark)

PS **2** Look at the pencils:

A

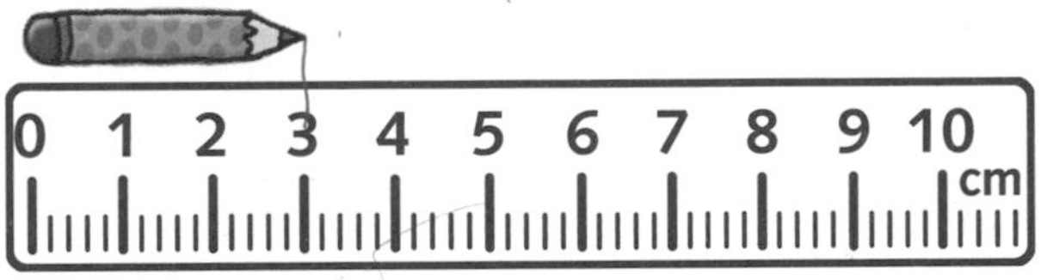
0 1 2 3 4 5 6 7 8 9 10
cm

B

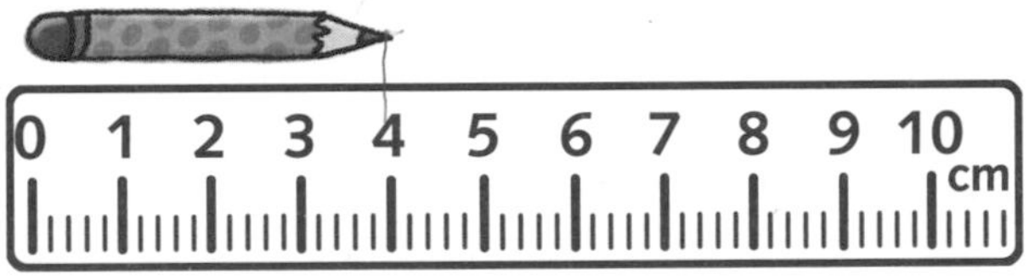
0 1 2 3 4 5 6 7 8 9 10
cm

**a)** Which pencil is longer? B ________ (1 mark)

**b)** What is its length? ________ 4 cm (1 mark)

**c)** How long would a pencil double this length be?

8 ________ 7 cm (1 mark)

**3** Write down two properties that describe these shapes as triangles.

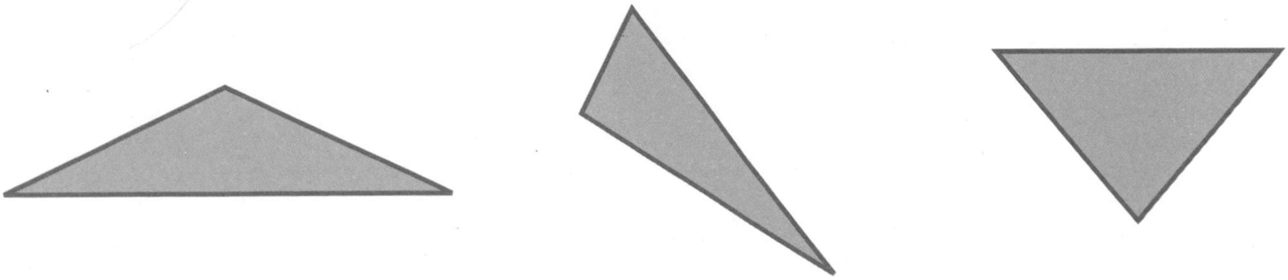

3 vertices

3 sides (2 marks)

**4** Complete this number pattern:

✓ 1, 2, 3, 3, 1, 2, _3_ , _3_ , _1_ , _2_ , _3_ , _3_

 1 mark

PS **5** Look at the circle. Imagine you are standing on **X**.

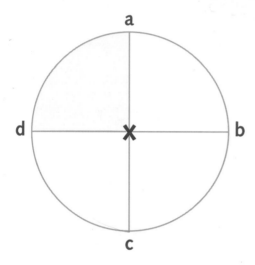

a
d **X** b
c

**a)** Face letter **a** and make an anti-clockwise quarter turn.

Which letter do you see? _____d_____

1 mark

**b)** Face letter **c** and make a half turn clockwise.

Which letter are you now facing? _____a_____

1 mark

**c)** What fraction of the circle is shaded?    $\frac{1}{4}$

1 mark

**6** Tick the 3-D shape that does not belong to the group.

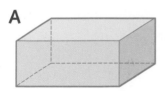
A

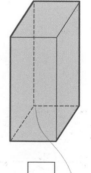
B    C

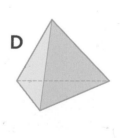
D

 ☐     ☐    ☐    ☑

1 mark

# Mixed Questions

7  Fill in the missing numbers.

a)

| 15 | 20 | 25 | 3⁰ | 35 | 40 | 45 | 50 |
|----|----|----|----|----|----|----|----|

1 mark

b)

| 99 | 89 | 79 | 69 | 59 | 49 | 39 | 29 |
|----|----|----|----|----|----|----|----|

1 mark

✓ c)

| 6 | 8 | 10 | 12 | 14 | 16 | 18 | 20 |
|---|---|----|----|----|----|----|----|

1 mark

8  Use the symbol <, > or = to compare the value of these numbers.

a)  19 [ < ] 56          1 mark

b)  27 [ = ] 27          1 mark

c)  35 [ > ] 14          1 mark

d)  99 [ < ] 143         1 mark

9  Look at the pictogram. It shows the snacks that some children brought to school.

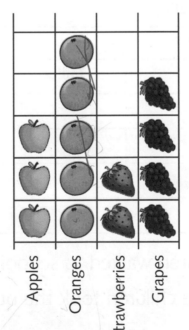

Key: 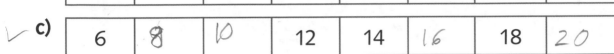 = 1 child brought an apple

Apples   Oranges   Strawberries   Grapes

a)  How many children brought strawberries?  ___2___      1 mark

b)  There are ___2___ more oranges than apples.           1 mark

What was the favourite snack?  ___orange___              1 mark

d)  How many snacks were brought altogether?  ___14___    1 mark

# Mixed Questions

**10** Write the correct time in words.

A          B          C          D

**a)** A = _half past three_                                      ☐ 1 mark

**b)** B = _quater to eight_                                       ☐ 1 mark

**c)** C = _quater past one_                                       ☐ 1 mark

**d)** D = _twelve o'clock_                                        ☐ 1 mark

PS **11** Look at the tally chart.

| How do we get to school? | |
|---|---|
| **Categories** | **Tallies** |
| Walk | IIII II   6 |
| Bike | III   3 |
| Car | IIII   4 |
| Bus | IIII IIII II |

**a)** How many children walked to school?        _7_        ☐ 1 mark

**b)** How many more children took the bus to school rather than the car?   12

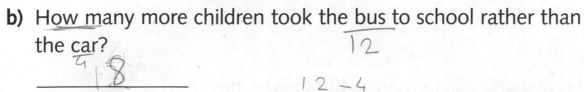

_8_                12 – 4                                  ☐ 1 mark

**c)** How many children were asked how they got to school?

_24_

# Mixed Questions

PS Problem-solving questions

**12** Janine has 10 sweets.

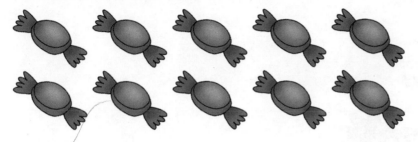

She eats six sweets.
How many are left? 4

1 mark

**13** Alan has 20 marbles.

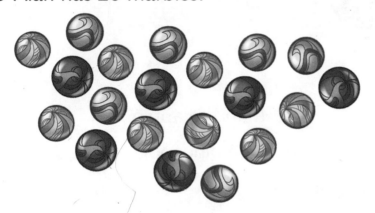

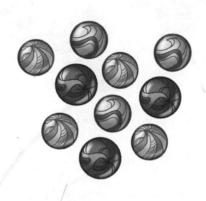

He finds 10 more marbles.
How many marbles does he have now? 30

1 mark

**14** Katie bought six new pairs of socks and Michael bought three new pairs of socks.

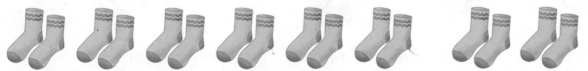

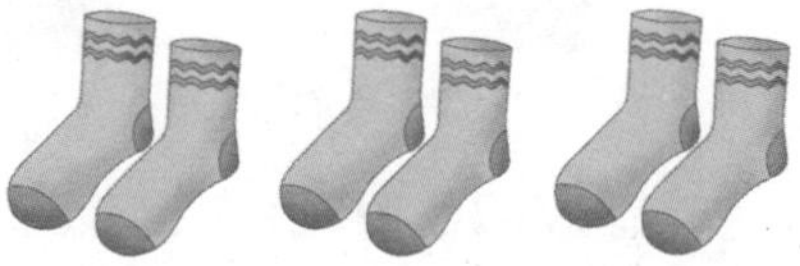

How many new pairs of socks were bought altogether? 9 pairs

1 mark

**15** Look at the picture and use the following words to make the sentences correct.

lighter    heavier

a)  The pineapple is ___heavier___ than the apple.

1 mark

b)  The apple is ___lighter___ than the pineapple.

1 mark

**PS** **16** Joshua and James have 10 juicy apples.

Divide them so that they each have the same number.

How many apples did they each get?

___5___

1 mark

**17** Complete the multiplications.

    **a)** $5 \times 2 =$ _____ 10 ____

    **b)** $7 \times 3 =$ _____ 21 ____

    **c)** $6 \times 10 =$ _____ 60 ____

    **d)** $10 \times 10 =$ _____ 100 ____

    **e)** $1 \times 5 =$ _____ 5 ____

    **f)** $9 \times 2 =$ _____ 18 ____

    **g)** $3 \times 5 =$ _____ 15 ____

    **h)** $5 \times 5 =$ _____ 25 ____

    **i)** $4 \times 10 =$ _____ 40 ____

    **j)** $8 \times 2 =$ _____ 16 ____

**18** Solve the following addition sums.

    **a)** $46 + 33 =$ _____ 79 ____

    **b)** $21 + 58 =$ _____ 79 ____

**19 a)** Colour $\frac{1}{4}$ of the circle.

    **b)** Colour $\frac{3}{4}$ of the square.

    **c)** Colour $\frac{1}{2}$ of the triangle.

1 mark (×15)

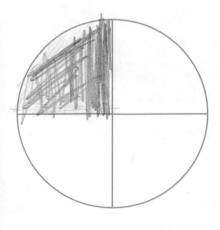

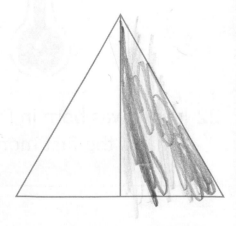

**20** Draw an array for:

**a)** 5 × 2

**b)** 10 × 5

2 marks

PS **21** What temperature does the thermometer show?

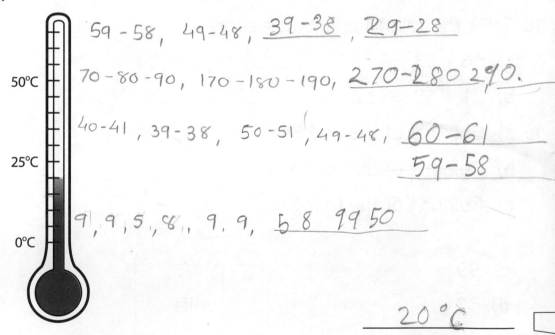

59 - 58,   49-48,   39-38 ,   29-28

70-80-90,   170-180-190,   270-280 290.

40-41 ,   39-38,   50-51 ,49-48,   60-61
59-58

9, 9, 5, 8, , 9, 9,   5 8  99 50

20 °C

1 mark

**22** Henry was born in December, the last month in the year.
What is the first month in the year?

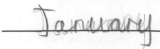
January

1 mark

# Mixed Questions

**23** What is the value of each set of coins?

**a)**              _15_          1 mark

**b)**              _16_          1 mark

**c)**              _28_          1 mark

**24** How much water is in each jug?

**a)**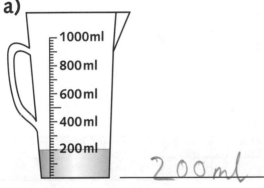

**b)**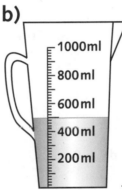

a) _200ml_          b) _500 ml_          2 marks

**25** Partition these two-digit numbers.

**a)** 46 = ___4___ tens ___6___ units          1 mark

**b)** 25 = ___2___ tens ___5___ units          1 mark

**c)** 99 = ___9___ tens ___9___ units          1 mark

**d)** 57 = ___5___ tens ___7___ units          1 mark

**26** Write these digits in words.

**a)** 9 ___nine___          1 mark

**b)** 30 ___thirty___          1 mark

**c)** 16 ___sixteen___          1 mark

**d)** 7 ___seven___          1 mark

# Answers

**Page 5 Quick Test**
1 **a)** four **b)** 13
2 16 = lowest value; 20 = highest value
3 1 2 3 4 5 6 7 8 **9** **10** 11 12 **13** **14** **15** 16 **17** 18 **19** **20**

**Page 7 Quick Test**
1 1 2 3 **4** **5** 6 **7** 8 **9** 10 **11** 12 **13** 14 15 **16** 17 **18** 19 **20**
2 **a)** 14 **b)** 8
3 1

**Page 9 Quick Test**
1 10
2 34 **44** **54** 64 **74** **84** 94
3 72 62 **52** **42** 32 **22** 12

**Page 11 Quick Test**
1

| 4 | 5 | 6 |

| 6 | 7 | 8 |

| 3 | 4 | 5 |

2 3, 19, 21, 35, 45
3 **a)** 16 > 9 **b)** 0 < 2 **c)** 98 > 32

**Page 12 Quick Test**
1 **a)** 60 + 5 **b)** 40 + 8 **c)** 10 + 3 **d)** 70 + 7
2 **a)** 35 **b)** 69 **c)** 51

**Page 13 Practice Questions**
**Challenge 1**
1 5 **10** 15 **20** 25 **30**

**Challenge 2**
1 **a)** 34 **b)** 67 **c)** 78 **d)** 99
2 2, 16, 23, 44, 54, 87, 100
3 23, 45, 5, 13

**Challenge 3**
1 **21** 18 **15** 12 **9** 6
2 **a)** 90 + 5 **b)** 10 + 7
3 Any number from:
 **a)** 24 to 32 **b)** 13 to 18

**Page 15 Quick Test**
1 Example: 4 + 6 = 10; 6 + 4 = 10; 10 − 6 = 4;
 10 − 4 = 6
2 **a)** 1 + 15 = 16 **b)** 20 = 10 + 10
 **c)** 23 − 5 = 18 **d)** 12 = 20 − 8

**Page 17 Quick Test**
1 **a)** 37 **b)** 91
2 **a)** 82 **b)** 72

**Page 18 Practice Questions**
**Challenge 1**
1 0 + 9; 1 + 8; 2 + 7; 3 + 6; 4 + 5; 9 + 0; 8 + 1;
 7 + 2; 6 + 3; 5 + 4

**Challenge 2**
1 10 − 4 = 6
2 10 + 10 = 20

**Challenge 3**
1 **a)** 9 + 1 = 10 **b)** 8 + 11 = 19
 **c)** 20 = 3 + 17 **d)** 14 = 5 + 9
2 10

**Page 19 Review Questions**
1 7
2 0, 3, 8, 17, 25, 54, 56, 69, 71
3 Group B
4 **a)** 20 + 3 **b)** 40 + 7
 **c)** 90 + 9 **d)** 10 + 3
5 94 **95** 96 **97** **98** 99 **100**

**Page 21 Quick Test**
1 **a)** 3 × 2 = 6
 **b)** 2 × 5 = 10
 **c)** 4 × 10 = 40

**Page 23 Quick Test**
1 **a)** 5
 **b)** 2
 **c)** 1
2 **a)** 10 ÷ 2 = 5 **b)** 10 ÷ 5 = 2 **c)** 10 ÷ 10 = 1

**Page 25 Quick Test**
1 8 × 2 = 16
2 8 ÷ 2 = 4
3

| | | | | | |
|---|---|---|---|---|---|
| | | | | | |
| | | | | | |

4 3, 5

**Page 26 Practice Questions**
**Challenge 1**
1

| 14 | 15 | 10 |
|---|---|---|
| 6 | 30 | 50 |
| 10 | 50 | 70 |
| 20 | 10 | 100 |

2 4 × 2 = 8; 4 ÷ 2 = 2

**Challenge 2**
1 5
2 **a)** 12 **b)** 6 × 2 = 12

**Challenge 3**
1 **a)** 5 × 2 = 10 **b)** 20 ÷ 4 = 5

**Page 27 Review Questions**
1 2, 10, 16, 17, 23, 45, 89, 98
2 **a)** 66, 67, 68 **b)** 44, 45, 46 **c)** 11, 12, 13
 **d)** 20, 21, 22 **e)** 29, 30, 31 **f)** 78, 79, 80

**3**  **a)**  14 < 16  **b)**  76 > 56  **c)**  23 < 25
   **d)**  89 > 34  **e)**  67 > 66  **f)**  88 < 99

**4**  **a)**  4 − 3 = 1  **b)**  14 + 6 = 20
   **c)**  23 − 7 = 16  **d)**  9 − 9 = 0

**5**  24, 26, 46, 42, 62, 64

## Page 29 Quick Test

**1**  **a)**  $\frac{1}{2}$  **b)**  $\frac{1}{4}$  **c)**  $\frac{3}{4}$

**2**  $\frac{1}{2}$

**3**  One whole or 1

## Page 31 Quick Test

**1**  Any suitable answers, e.g.

**2**  Any suitable answers, e.g.

**3**  Any suitable answers, e.g.

**4**  **a)**  1
   **b)**  2

## Page 33 Quick Test

**1**  8
**2**  4
**3**  12
**4**  8

## Page 34 Practice Questions
### Challenge 1

**1**  **a)**  Block C
   **b)**  Block A
   **c)**  Block B

### Challenge 2

**1**  $\frac{4}{4}$

**2**  $\frac{3}{4}$

**3**  $\frac{1}{2}$

**4**  $\frac{1}{2}$

### Challenge 3

**1**  **a)**  4
   **b)**  2
   **c)**  $\frac{3}{4}$

## Page 35 Review Questions

**1**  **a)**  10  **b)**  10  **c)**  50
**2**  3 × 2 = 6
**3**  **a)**  4  **b)**  3  **c)**  10
**4**  6 ÷ 2 = 3
**5**  5 × 2 = 10
**6**  **a)**  10  **b)**  20  **c)**  24
**7**  **a)**  3  **b)**  7  **c)**  8

## Page 37 Quick Test

**1**  500 g
**2**  600 ml
**3**  4 cm

## Page 39 Quick Test

**1**

**2**  Thursday
**3**  April, May, June, July, August, September, October, November, December

## Page 41 Quick Test

**1**  Any suitable combinations, e.g.

**2**  **a)**  8p change  **b)**  0p change
   **c)**  4p change

## Page 42 Practice Questions
### Challenge 1

**1**  B, C, A (8 cm, 13 cm, 20 cm)
**2**  **a)**  300 ml  **b)**  800 ml

# Answers

**Challenge 2**
1 87p
2 13p

**Challenge 3**
1 quarter to three
2 quarter past two

## Page 43 Review Questions
1 a) $\frac{1}{2}$ b) $\frac{1}{4}$ c) $\frac{3}{4}$
2 5
3 7
4 $1\frac{1}{4}$
5 8
6 $2\frac{1}{4}$
7 a) 4
 b) 2
8 8

## Page 45 Quick Test
1 rectangle
2 Any two: 5 faces, 5 vertices, 8 edges
3 sphere
4 E

## Page 47 Quick Test
1 a)
 b)
 c)
 d)
 e)

2 candle, pencil, food tin are just some examples of cylinder shapes

## Page 48 Practice Questions
**Challenge 1**
1 a) pentagon b) circle c) rectangle
2 hexagon

**Challenge 2**
1 a) sphere b) pyramid c) cone
2 Any two: 8 vertices, 6 faces, 12 edges
3 cylinder

**Challenge 3**
1 Any suitable answers, e.g.

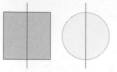

2
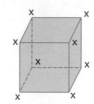

## Page 49 Review Questions
1 a) i) A = 8 cm ii) B = 6 cm
 b) 14 cm
2 a) 200 ml
 b) 400 ml
3 half past three
4 £1.80

## Page 51 Quick Test
1

2 clockwise

## Page 53 Quick Test
1 Move forward one.
2 Make a quarter turn clockwise.
3 Move forward five to land on the coin.
4 Make a half turn clockwise or anti-clockwise.
5 Move forward three.
6 Make a quarter turn clockwise.
7 Move forward three to get to the house.

**Page 54 Practice Questions**
**Challenge 1**
1   yellow, green
2   6 6 6, 10 10 10
3   anti-clockwise

**Challenge 2**
1   anti-clockwise
2   A quarter turn anti-clockwise

**Challenge 3**
1   5–4, 5–6
2   add 3 each time
3   10

**Page 55 Review Questions**
1   **a)** cube   **b)** cuboid   **c)** cylinder
2   Any two: 5 vertices, 8 edges, 5 faces
3   cuboid
4   **a)** hexagon   **b)** triangle   **c)** square
5   Any suitable answers, e.g.

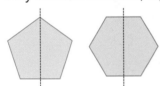

6   triangle
7   triangle and square

**Page 57 Quick Test**
1   **a)** brown
    **b)** 35
    **c)**

| Coloured snail | Tally |
|---|---|
| Grey | 卌 卌 卌 卌 |
| White | 卌 卌 卌 |
| Orange | 卌 卌 |
| Brown | 卌 卌 卌 卌 卌 |

**Page 59 Quick Test**
1   **a)** 5
    **b)** 8
    **c)** 7
    **d)** 20

**Page 60 Practice Questions**
**Challenge 1**
1

| Sweets | Tally |
|---|---|
| 🍬🍬🍬🍬🍬🍬 🍬🍬🍬🍬🍬🍬 | 卌 卌 II |
| 🍬🍬🍬🍬🍬🍬🍬 | 卌 II |
| 🍬🍬🍬 | III |

**Challenge 2**
1   **a)** 5
    **b)** 2
    **c)** 15

**Challenge 3**
1   **a)** 7 minutes
    **b)** 12 minutes

**Page 61 Review Questions**
1   **a)** apple
    **b)** teddy
    **c)** beaker and sandwich
    **d)** banana
2   **a)**            **b)**

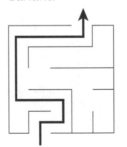 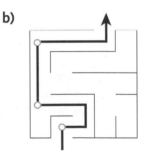

    **c)**

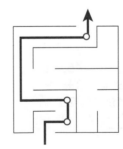

75

# Answers

**3** a)–e)

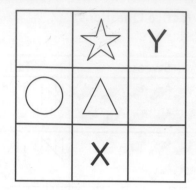

## Page 62 Review Questions

**1** a) 12
b) 17
c) 36

**2**

| Bird | Tally |
|------|-------|
| Blackbird |卌 ||| |
| Robin | ||| |
| Sparrow | 卌 卌 | |

**3** a) 15 cm
b) 30 cm
c) weeks 3 and 4 (it grew 20 cm)

## Mixed Questions pages 63–71

**1** a) 2
b) 4
c) 6
**2** a) B
b) 4 cm
c) 8 cm
**3** 3 corners, 3 sides
**4** 3, 3, 1, 2, 3, 3
**5** a) d
b) a
c) $\frac{1}{4}$
**6** D (the pyramid)
**7** a) 15, **20**, 25, **30**, 35, 40, **45**, **50**
b) 99, 89, 79, **69**, **59**, **49**, **39**, 29
c) 6, **8**, **10**, 12, 14, **16**, 18, **20**
**8** a) 19 < 56 b) 27 = 27 c) 35 > 14
d) 99 < 143
**9** a) 2 b) 2 c) oranges d) 14
**10** a) A = half past three
b) B = a quarter to eight
c) C = quarter past one
d) D = 12 o'clock
**11** a) 7 b) 8 c) 26
**12** 4
**13** 30
**14** 9

**15** a) The pineapple is **heavier** than the apple.
b) The apple is **lighter** than the pineapple.
**16** 5
**17** a) 10 b) 21 c) 60 d) 100 e) 5
f) 18 g) 15 h) 25 i) 40 j) 16
**18** a) 79 b) 79
**19** Any suitable answers, e.g.
a)

b)
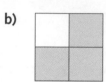

c)
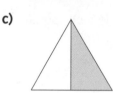

**20** a) 5 x 2 =   xx
xx
xx
xx
xx
b) 10 x 5 =   xxxxx
xxxxx
xxxxx
xxxxx
xxxxx
xxxxx
xxxxx
xxxxx
xxxxx
xxxxx
**21** 20°C
**22** January
**23** a) 15p b) 16p c) 28p
**24** a) 200 ml b) 500 ml
**25** a) 46 = 4 tens 6 units
b) 25 = 2 tens 5 units
c) 99 = 9 tens 9 units
d) 57 = 5 tens 7 units
**26** a) nine b) thirty c) sixteen d) seven

| | |
|---|---|
| **2-D shape** | A shape that only has two dimensions (such as width and height) and no thickness. A flat shape. |
| **3-D shape** | An object that has height, width and depth, like any object in the real world. A solid shape. |

**A**

| | |
|---|---|
| **Alternate** | To miss out every other number. |
| **Amount** | The sum total. |
| **Anti-clockwise** | The opposite direction to which the hands on a clock move in. |
| **Array** | An order or arrangement of objects. |

**B**

| | |
|---|---|
| **Backwards** | The reverse of forwards. |
| **Block graph** | A graph that shows numbers or amounts as rectangles of different sizes. |
| **Bottom** | The lowest part of something. |

**C**

| | |
|---|---|
| **Calculation** | Working something out (by +, −, ×, ÷). |
| **Capacity** | The maximum amount of liquid that can be contained (measured in litres (l) and millilitres (ml)). |
| **Centimetre** | A unit for measuring length (cm). |
| **Chart** | A list, drawing or graph showing data in a way that is easy to understand. |
| **Chronological** | Arranged or described in order of time. |
| **Clockwise** | The direction the hands move on a clock. |
| **Coin** | A piece of money made from metal. |
| **Combination** | Putting, using or mixing things together. |
| **Corner** | Where two sides meet. |

| | |
|---|---|
| **Count** | Say how many there are. Say numbers in order. |
| **Currency** | The system of money used in a country. |

**D**

| | |
|---|---|
| **Data** | Facts or information. |
| **Denominator** | The number that is below the line in a fraction and tells you how many parts are in the whole. |
| **Different** | Unlike another. |
| **Digit** | One of the written numbers 0–9. |
| **Direction** | The path that someone or something moves upon. |
| **Divide** | A calculation to find out how many times a large number contains a small number. |
| **Double** | Twice as many; multiplied by 2. |

**E**

| | |
|---|---|
| **Edge** | Where two faces of a 3-D shape meet. |
| **Equal** | The same in amount, number or size. |
| **Equally** | In equal amounts. |
| **Equivalent** | Having the same amount, value, purpose or qualities. |
| **Even (number)** | Forming a whole number that can be divided exactly by 2. |

**F**

| | |
|---|---|
| **Face** | An individual surface of a 3-D shape. |
| **Fact** | A pair of numbers that equal an amount (for example $1 + 9 = 10$, $2 + 8 = 10$, etc.) |
| **Factor** | Numbers you can multiply together to get another number. |
| **Flat shape** | Another name for a 2-D shape. |
| **Forwards** | When counting, move from a lower value number to a higher value number; to move in the direction you are facing. |
| **Fraction** | A part of a whole object group of objects or a |

**G**

| | |
|---|---|
| **Gram** | A metric unit of mass (weight). |
| **Graph** | A diagram of values, usually shown as lines or bars. |
| **Group** | A number of people or things that are put together or considered as a unit. |

**H**

| | |
|---|---|
| **Half** | One of two equal parts of a whole. |
| **Half past** | Half past a particular hour is 30 minutes later than that hour. |
| **Half turn** | To make part of a turn. A full turn is made up of two equal half turns. |
| **Halve/d** | To divide something into two equal pieces. |
| **Higher** | Greater than the usual level or amount. |
| **Hour** | A period of time equal to $\frac{1}{24}$ (a twenty-fourth) of a day. |

**I**

| | |
|---|---|
| **Information** | Facts about a person, event or situation. |
| **Inverse** | Opposite (the reverse of). |

**K**

| | |
|---|---|
| **Kilogram** | A unit (kg) of mass equal to 1000 grams. |

**L**

| | |
|---|---|
| **Larger** | Big in size or amount. |
| **Length** | The measurement of something from end to end or along its longest side. |
| **Less** | A smaller amount. |
| **Litre** | A unit (l) for measuring the volume of liquid. |
| **Lots of** | The same amounts of (for example two lots of 10). |
| **Lower** | To reduce the amount of something or to position something below. |

**M**

| | |
|---|---|
| **Mass** | Mass is commonly measured by how much something weighs (measured in grams (g) and kilograms (kg)). |
| **Metre** | The basic unit (m) of length (or distance) in the metric system. |
| **Middle** | Positioned in the centre. |
| **Millilitre** | A metric unit (ml) of volume. |
| **Minute** | Period of time totalling 60 seconds. There are 60 minutes in one hour. |
| **More** | A larger amount. |

**N**

| | |
|---|---|
| **Note** | A piece of money made from paper. |
| **Number** | Quantity or amount represented by a word or symbol |
| **Numerator** | The top number in a fraction; shows how many parts of the whole you have. |

**O**

| | |
|---|---|
| **O'clock** | The time when the long hand is pointing at the 12. |
| **Odd (number)** | Any number that cannot be divided exactly by 2. |
| **Operation** | A mathematical process (usually +, −, ×, ÷). |
| **Order** | Putting things into their correct place following some rule. |

**P**

| | |
|---|---|
| **Pair** | Two of a kind. |
| **Partitioning** | Splitting a number into parts (for example 10s and units). |
| **Pattern** | Things that are arranged following a rule/rules. |
| **Pence** | A unit of money used in the UK. There are 100 pence in a pound. |
| **Pictogram** | A pictogram uses pictures or symbols to show the value of the data. |
| **Place value** | The value of a digit depending on its place within a number. |

| | |
|---|---|
| **Pounds** | A unit of money used in the UK. A pound is equal to 100 pence. |
| **Problem** | A question that needs a solution. |
| **Product** | The answer when two or more numbers are multiplied together. |
| **Properties** | Characteristics that something has, such as colour, height, weight, etc. |

**Q**

| | |
|---|---|
| **Quartered** | To split something into four equal parts. |
| **Quarter past** | 15 minutes past the hour. |
| **Quarter to** | 15 minutes to the hour. |
| **Quarter turn** | To make a part (quarter) of a turn. Also, another name for a right-angle turn. |

**R**

| | |
|---|---|
| **Regular** | Usual or ordinary. In shapes, when all the sides and angles are the same. |
| **Repeated** | Shown or done again. |
| **Right-angle turn** | A 90° turn or quarter turn. |
| **Rotation** | A circular movement. There is a central point that stays fixed and everything else moves around that point in a circle. |

**S**

| | |
|---|---|
| **Same** | Exactly like another. |
| **Second** | A short unit of time. |
| **Sequence** | A list of numbers or objects in a special order. |
| **Scale** | The numbers that show the units on a graph. |
| **Shape** | The form of an object (how it is laid out in space). |
| **Share** | Splitting into equal parts, amounts or groups. |
| **Smaller** | Little in size or amount when compared to another. |

| | |
|---|---|
| **Solid** | A three-dimensional (3-D) object with width, depth and height. |
| **Step** | A stage in a process. |
| **Symmetry/ Symmetrical** | Symmetry is when one shape becomes exactly like another if you flip, slide or turn it. |

**T**

| | |
|---|---|
| **Table** | Numbers or quantities arranged in rows and columns. |
| **Tally** | A record or count of a number of things. |
| **Tally chart** | A chart used to show data visually. A tally chart counts in lots of 5. |
| **Three-quarter turn** | To turn three equal parts out of four in a clockwise or anti-clockwise direction. |
| **Top** | The highest place or part. |
| **Total** | The result of adding. |

**U**

| | |
|---|---|
| **Units** | The first position in place value. A single-digit number. |

**V**

| | |
|---|---|
| **Value** | How much something is worth. |
| **Vertex (vertices)** | A point (or points) where two or more straight lines meet. A corner. |

**W**

| | |
|---|---|
| **Weight** | How heavy something is. |
| **Whole** | All of something. |
| **Worth** | Having a particular value. |

# Index